# PLANT BASED DIET

*The revolutionary diet book with easy and tasty recipes for healthy and smart people!*

By

**Richard McWhites.**

# TABLE OF CONTENTS

# INTRODUCTION

A whole lot of people never give eating healthy to lose weight a try for a number of reasons. They claim they don't have the time or the willpower, or they just don't like healthy food, or being fat is their natural body makeup, or they're too tired. Some even blame it on the weather. If they have cold winters, they say they can't lose weight because it's too cold. If they have hot summers, they say it's too hot. Some say they don't have time even though it takes the same amount of time to eat unhealthy as it does to eat healthy. Then some have simply never learned how to eat healthy to lose weight

There are no doubt, hundreds of excuses people use to avoid healthy eating. You and I know these are merely excuses. If some people can eat healthy, there's really no reason everybody can't eat healthy.

Healthy eating is all about being full of energy and keeping yourself fit. It does not mean that you need to hold yourself back from eating the food you love. It is just about eating the right quantity at the right time.

Healthy eating does not only mean what to eat but also how to eat. In a way, it means smart eating. Right choice of food is very important as it helps in reducing risk of problems like diabetes, heart problems, cancer, depression, etc. It even helps in strengthening your memory.

What if one simple change could put you on a path to better health? And what if that change could even save you from obesity, heart disease and cancer? You have the power to transform your life by maintaining a plant based diet - no ifs about it.

"As I see skyrocketing incidences of conditions such as diabetes, hypertension, and heart disease, I am profoundly aware that there is so much

potential for preventing or even reversing most of these problems through very inexpensive lifestyle changes centered on proper nutrition."
— Carmelo Mejia, MD, Internal Medicine, Kaiser Permanente

While many omnivores feel that a meal without meat just doesn't feel like a meal, the vegan and vegetarian plant based lifestyle is growing in popularity just the same - and with good reason. A plant based diet moves away from animal-based foods like meat, eggs and milk, and incorporates more fruit, vegetables, legumes and grains. The less meat and dairy you eat the less fat you take in. This goes a long way when it comes to maintaining healthy weight and cholesterol levels.

The secret to great health is simple. It doesn't mean spending hours suffering at the gym. It doesn't mean giving up girls' nights or social events. It doesn't mean juicing for 30 days or trying a new diet every 6 months. It doesn't come in pill form.

It means eating a plant-based diet.

A plant-based diet doesn't necessarily mean being vegan (although it can), it just means that the majority of every meal comes from the ground, is whole, and unprocessed. It's about exploring and discovering the joys of whole foods in their natural state and using them to elevate your health to new heights.

Great health means waking up well rested, going through the day free of distracting cravings, having a strong immune system, feeling energized to do things that are good for you like working out, taking a yoga class or two and then being able to enjoy quality time with friends and family. A plant-based diet supports and enhances all of this.

## Why Should The Majority Of What We Eat Come From The Ground?

Eating more plants is the only nutritional protocol known to man to prevent and even reverse the chronic illnesses that ravage our society. Plants and vegetables are full of macro and micronutrients that provide our bodies with everything we need for a healthy and vibrant life. By eating at least two meals packed with veggies every day, and snacking on fruits and veggies in between, the quality of your health and ultimately your life will drastically improve.

The most common health concerns that people have can be alleviated by this one simple step. Things like obesity, poor sleep, bad skin, accelerated aging, inflammation, physical pain, and lack of energy can all be positively affected by increasing the intake of plants and natural foods. As a society, we've come to accept that common discomforts like headaches, constant fatigue, PMS, and aches and pains are just part of life. We grumble through them and maybe turn to the pharmacy for relief, but what we end up doing is muting the message our bodies are trying to send to us. A good majority of the time these are signs of a nutrient deficiency.

Additionally, when we increase consumption of plant foods, we reduce our intake of processed foods that impede our bodies' ability to function at its highest potential. This enables better waste elimination, flushes toxins, and enhances nutrient absorption.

# WHAT IS A PLANT BASED DIET?

A plant based diet is a diet where you only eat foods that come out of the ground and have not been processed in any way. The foods are generally consumed raw, but you can enjoy a lightly cooked meal at the end of the day.

A plant based diet consists of fruit, vegetables, nuts, and seeds. Each of these contains all the essential nutrients that the human body needs to promote healthy digestion, cell function and repair, heart health, bone health, and even mental health. At the same time, they are low in calories, fat, and cholesterol. They help in maintaining weight while providing adequate amounts of fiber, vitamins, carbohydrates, and antioxidants.

The way to ensure there is an adequate supply of all the nutrients needed to have a healthy disposition is to vary up the plant based foods that are eaten. There are several to choose from so the possibilities for variety are better than one would expect. The diet does include salads and fresh fruit, but also consists of whole grain products, beans, oils, herbs and spices. All together, these items can be mixed and matched and prepared in various ways to get the amounts of nutrients needed for good health, without necessarily having to take supplements.

Plant based foods contain amino acids, various vitamins, protein, fiber and magnesium, an absolutely vital nutrient for good health, among others. They can be found in several foods. Some foods contain a lot of some nutrients and only a little of others, which is why variety is highly recommended for a plant based diet. Here are a few nutrients that need to be in adequate supply from food, and it is important to look out for and try to consume them at every meal.

Calcium is one nutrient the human body needs for strong teeth and bones, but it is not made or stored within the human body. To get an adequate supply of calcium, leafy greens must be a main staple of a plant based diet. These include spinach, kale, bok choy, collard, mustard and turnip greens. Almonds and hazelnuts can be added to a meal for a little extra calcium.

Iron is very important in the transport of oxygen to the organs in the body. Leafy greens are a good source of iron, but other items will provide the necessary iron as well. In order to consume enough iron on a plant based diet, foods like oatmeal, whole wheat breads, and lentils, along with several other foods. Iron rich foods should be consumed on a regular basis.

Vitamin B12 is one vitamin we need, but is not very abundant in plant based diets. B12 can be found in fortified foods and supplements. This essential vitamin plays a part in giving us energy, reduces the risk of several diseases, and helps with overall mental health, so it needs to be a regular part of the plant based diet.

The foods of the earth in their natural form are unaltered and therefore healthier for humans than animal based and cooked foods. With a bit of research and the implementation of variety, a person could successfully achieve great health and a well balanced lifestyle by adopting a plant based diet.

# WHAT WILL YOU ACHIEVE WITH A PLANT BASED DIET?

The plant based diet is not another fad diet because you can make it a permanent part of your life and reap many health benefits along with it. Studies have shown that this diet can help you to enjoy a long and healthy life.

**Below Are Proven Health Benefits Of A Plant Based Diet.**

- Boost Immune System

Did you know that about 80% of your immune system is situated in your digestive system? Thus if your digestive system is clogged, then your immune system will be down and you will be susceptible to all kinds of diseases and common ailments.

Plants are high in fiber, and when it passes through your digestive system, it latches on to all the gunk that has built up along the sides of your intestinal wall and eliminates it from the body. Once all this buildup is removed from your body, your immune system can function normal again and protect you against allergies, the common cold and autoimmune disorders such as HIV.

- Blood Sugar

A highly effective method to control high blood sugar is to increase the fiber in the diet. A fiber-rich diet is perfect to help with slowing the absorption of sugar in the bloodstream. An added benefit is the ability to control hunger throughout the course of the day. Also, fiber can help with balancing the level of cortisol in the blood stream, which is responsible for the feelings of stress. Many of the animal foods can have a significant hand in increasing the blood sugar level.

- Weight Loss

A diet consisting of plant-based and whole foods, with minimal processed sugars and low in fat, is certain to help with cutting weight. A further benefit comes from a diet that is high in clean and raw whole foods. Weight loss is naturally able to occur when the daily diet includes a higher percentage of vitamins, minerals, and fiber compared to proteins and animal fats. A well-planned plant-based diet has the potential to cut 4-6 pounds within a two-week period. This should also ensure you aren't left feeling hungry.

- Prevent Cancer

A plant based diet can also protect you against all types of cancers. This is because most plants are high in antioxidants which help the body to get rid of toxins which cause the cells in your body to become cancerous.

- Blood pressure

A plant-based diet offers a perfect source of potassium-rich foods which can help to naturally lower blood pressure. Fruits and vegetables, as well as most seeds, nuts, legumes, and whole grain include a sufficient amount of vitamin B6 and potassium for healthy blood pressure. Animal foods like meat include minimal potassium and can lead to higher cholesterol and blood pressure.

- Cholesterol

A significant benefit of adopting a plant-based diet is the ability to lower cholesterol. Plants are cholesterol-free, even the more saturated types like cacao and coconut. For this reason, eating a diet that mostly consists of plant-based foods can offer a simple solution to lowering cholesterol. Great food choices to lower rates of heart disease and cholesterol include seeds, nuts, whole grains, fruits, and vegetables.

- Anti-Aging

The diet also helps to protect you from the free radicals that contribute to aging. According to studies, free radicals are the number one cause of aging both internally and externally. Therefore the diet can help you to avoid age related diseases, and keep you looking and feeling young. But not only will the diet protect your physical being, but your mind will also be able to remain young and strong.

# PLANT BASED OR VEGAN? WHY ARE YOU WRONG...

An often heard word when people discuss or mention their eating or dietary preferences is the term "vegan." And, some say they only consume a plant-based diet. While they may seem similar, there are some subtle differences between the two. We are going to make a comparison of a plant-based diet vs. vegan to see if they are the same or different.

Read on to know more about these diets so that you will be able to identify the types of food in each of these dietary choices.

If you think that a plant-based diet and vegan diet are the same, then you are wrong. Don't worry, you are not alone. In fact, there are many people who consider them to be the same and even use these terms interchangeably. People seem to get confused between a plant-based diet and a vegan diet. And, a few them even think that vegan is just another word for a plant-based diet.

According to The Vegan Society, "Veganism is a way of living which seeks to exclude, as far as is possible and practicable, all forms of exploitation of, and cruelty to, animals for food, clothing, or any other purpose."

So, being a vegan is not just what you eat, but in fact, a lifestyle which you adopt. A vegan avoids anything that has an animal source like honey, eggs, milk, silk, wool, and more. A vegan diet, on the other hand, is completely free from animal exploitation.

Since vegans only have access to plant proteins, they can miss out on essential amino acids. To overcome this issue, a vegan would need to make a combination of pulses using beans, chickpeas, and grains. This combination should be included in different meals.

Baked beans on toast, rice with pulses, or lentils with bread could be a good combo. Regular inclusion of beans, chickpeas, lentils, and nuts in the diet can help to overcome most of the nutritional deficiencies that vegan people face.

Furthermore, vitamin B12 is found only in animal products. So, vegans are recommended to take a vitamin B12 supplement.

A plant-based diet is favored among nutritionists and celebrities. Eggs, milk, honey, and other animal products are allowed in a plant-based diet, so it is not solely a plant-only diet.

# Why A Plant-Based Diet Is Healthier Than Vegan Diet

There is an overlap between a plant-based diet and a vegan diet. But overall, a plant-based diet is easier and flexible.

It is even considered to be a healthier option that focuses on nutrient-dense foods rather than processed food. Also, since dairy products and eggs are part of this diet, the issue related to the lack of complete proteins or vitamin B12 is much less.

So, there is a huge difference between a plant-based diet and vegan diet. And, going vegan is not the same as adopting a plant-based diet.

The plant-based diet focuses on eating healthy and is more inclined towards eating whole grains, pulses, and sprouts. Since other plant-based products like soy milk and plant-based items do not supply all the essential proteins, plant-based diet followers eat a lot of sprouts and pulses to reach the daily required amount of proteins.

Vegans, on the other hand, prefer foods like fruits, vegetables, grains, beans, nuts, and seeds.

# IT MATTERS!

There is not much mystery about a 'plant-based diet' but it may be interesting to ponder for a little on the vastness of what it holds for you.

- Whole Foods

Firstly, a plant-based diet recognizes the value of natural, whole foods, not nutrients or calories, as the fundamental unit of nutrition. This is due to the synergistic combination of vitamins, minerals, antioxidants and phytochemicals that can only take place with whole foods. Thus it makes good food sense to have moderate amounts of different whole foods in your diet all the time.

This continual switching around of one type of vegetable, whole grain or fruit for another till you have all the different types of phytochemicals well inside your body is very important for ultimate health. Besides, different parts of your body require different plant chemicals to function; thus, a healthy mix of nutrients is essential to good health.

- Colors of Natural Foods

Further, a plant-based diet is also about eating the colors. Combining different colors and types of fruits and vegetables is both healthy and appetizing. In fact, colors give clues to the nutrients they contain.

For example, red indicates vitamin A (beta carotene) and vitamin C. Closely following, is yellow, which is a sign of potassium and fiber; while green means it is packed with iron or folic acid. Further, blue and purple colors show the presence of anthocyanins that fight free radicals; and white shines with vitamins and minerals.

- Healing Power of Foods

Notably, the healing power of whole foods in a plant-based diet is at your disposal if you care to use it. However, this sort of healing is seldom instantaneous; Nature must be allowed to take its course and there are no health miracles overnight.

Meanwhile, the processed foods in your diet can cancel out all the good work of natural foods in the blink of an eye. What you do and do not eat are all important if you wish to see definite results.

- Green Blood of Plants

In a way, a plant-based diet is letting in the sun in your life when you eat leafy greens with a high amount of chlorophyll. In fact, your own red blood thrives on the green blood of plants. So, the more greens you have inside your body, the more oxygen to produce red blood cells for you. Just as the trees depend on the leaves for food, you can make it through life with leafy greens.

- Food Preparation

Lastly, a plant-based diet takes into consideration the way foods are prepared or eaten; so you should feed on fresh foods or freshly cooked food. There was a case in which re-heated leftovers were served to a woman in confinement. From that time onwards, her health went downhill and she lost all her energy, not being able to hold down any full-time job.

Thus, Wordsworth had been right all along - that there is a close bond between man and nature. And a plant-based diet is the nearest thing though it may not be exactly what the dear poet had in mind.

# HOW TO USE HEALTHY FOODS TO LOSE WEIGHT - WILL A PLANT BASED DIET WORK?

My experience chasing weight loss is probably not much different than most people. I have worked at weight loss and weight management for most of my adult life. I'm now sixty years old. There was a time when I tried all kinds of the newest and latest methods to loss weight quickly, I have used pre-scripted diets, diet products, even eating habits therapy. I could usually make some progress and lose some weight, but I have always found that unless I stayed with the program permanently I would just go back to where I was. I found that most of these diets and diet products, were not a good recipe for my health. I also love good food, I like to cook and as I have gotten older, above all, I want to be as healthy as possible.

I am a firm believer that good health and long term health management is rooted in nutrition and a balanced well chosen food group as well as a consistent exercise regiment. Weight loss, weight management and great health all go together. Once I got this clearly embedded in my brain, I realized that the basis of this thinking was really pretty simple.

Eat real fresh food, mostly plants. I am not advocating a vegetarian diet here, I personally am not a practicing vegetarian. I do think a well thought out and practiced vegetarian diet can be great for weight loss and excellent health.

When I say eat real fresh food, it's that simple. Stay away from manufactured, highly processed foods. If you have put any thought into why there is an out of control obesity epidemic in the U.S. and you put two and two together, you realize it is rooted in two factors. A lack of real fresh food and sedentary lifestyles. Little to no exercise.

The plant based diet is not about only eating plants, like fruits and vegetables. Include fish, chicken and other meats if you want to eat them, the key is moderation.

Eat at least an 80 % plant based diet. Most foods like nuts, grains, beans, sweet potatoes etc., are all plant based foods.

**Eat Only Fresh Fruits And Lightly Cook Your Vegetables.**

You need all the nutrition and enzymes you can get from the plant based foods you eat. When you over cook your vegetables you lose a lot of the nutrition and eliminate the beneficial enzymes. Along with the lightly cooked vegetables also eat some fruits and vegetables raw each day. Salads are great but also consider making a green drink. Here's is a simple recipe I make almost everyday. Take a blender or better if you have it or can buy one, a Vita Mix or other high speed blender. Put in a hand full of fresh kale, a small bunch of fresh Italian parsley, a sprig of celery, maybe a small chunk of cabbage, one or two cored apples, one or two cored pears and a wedge of lemon with the peel on.. Put in more than one apple and pear for how sweet you want it, you can also play around with different fruits, sometimes I also put in berries, like blue berries. This green drink does not taste like it may look, the fruit mixed with the vegetables gives it a slightly sweet pleasant taste. The idea here is you get a big shot of fresh, raw vegetables and fruit, with very low caloric content and tons of nutritional and antioxidant content and fiber. This is a super healthy all fresh plant based weight loss drink.

Losing weight and getting really healthy is really all about changing your food consciousness, eating an unadulterated diet. I mean that the food you are eating has not gone through any manufacturing or heavy processing. The grains you eat are not refined, choose brown rice rather than white rice, whole grain pasta (only very occasionally) chose sweet potatoes over regular white russet type potatoes. The idea here is two avoid foods that immediately turn into sugar in your system.

When you eat meats or fish, eat small portions and avoid rich sauces, tons of butter or other dairy based condiments. For adding taste to any cooked food you eat, use herbs, garlic, coconut oil or virgin olive oil also possibly grape seed oil is OK. Stay away from most other oils. Don't over eat any dairy products, go for almond milk rather than cows milk, limit cheeses and butter. Consider yogurt rather than creme when cooking and stay clear of all refined sugars..

Beware of the food like substances, like high fructose corn syrup, trans fats, hydrogenated oils, too much sugar, too much salt, lots of preservatives and other chemicals. These are the culprits that are in most of the processed, refined and packaged foods in the average mainstream market.

Look for and join a co-op natural foods market, or any kind of natural foods market. Go to a local outdoor Sat. market to shop.

Try changing when you eat. Eat small meals more often and don't eat a meal after say 4 or 5 PM, if you want a snack later eat a piece of fruit. Take a walk after your last meal. Sitting on the couch after a large meal and then going off to bed will put on the weight and keep it.

This concept for being a nutrition and fresh food conscious eater is at the heart of losing weight and being in excellent health. It may be a big change for many people and habits are the hardest parts of our daily lives to change. Take it a step at a time and stay focused, put time into it, educate yourself, it is well worth it.

# SUPER PLANT BASED DIET RECIPES FOR SMART PEOPLE

## BREAKFAST

For those who have recently adopted a whole food plant-based (WFPB) diet, there seems to be a misconception that oatmeal is the only heart-healthy breakfast available.

That causes concern because, though oatmeal is good, it can quickly become boring if eaten seven days a week.

We know breakfast is important. It has been called the most important meal of the day for a number of reasons.

Need some breakfast inspiration? Bored with your current morning routine? Maybe you're looking for a plant-based version of a longtime fave?

There's something for everyone in these fabulous whole-food, plant-based breakfast recipes.

- Orange French Toast

Aquafaba is the not-so-secret ingredient that make this vegan French toast recipe soft, thick, and eggy—without the eggs. Use your favorite bread or berries to create your own signature version.

Aquafaba is the liquid that comes from soaking or cooking beans or legumes— it's the thick liquid you see when you open a can of chickpeas. The liquid is often used in vegan baked goods as an egg substitute, as its texture and composition of starches and protein make it useful for thickening, binding, emulsifying, and foaming.

You can use the liquid from canned or boxed chickpeas or other beans, or make your own.

Headnote: Use a large nonstick griddle to make the French toast in batches. The texture of the toast will depend on which kind of bread you select. Denser breads will need to be soaked a bit longer than softer breads.

Total time: 30min

Serves: 8

**Ingredients**

FRENCH TOAST

- ✓ 1 ½ cup unsweetened, unflavored plant milk
- ✓ ½ cup almond flour
- ✓ 1 cup aquafaba
- ✓ 2 tablespoons pure maple syrup
- ✓ ¼ teaspoon ground cinnamon
- ✓ 2 pinches of salt (optional)
- ✓ ½ tablespoon orange zest (from half an orange)
- ✓ 8 whole-grain bread slices (about ¾ inches thick)

# BERRY COMPOTE

- ✓ 4.5 ounces (about 1 cup) blueberries or raspberries (fresh, or frozen and thawed)
- ✓ ½ cup applesauce
- ✓ 1 teaspoon pure maple syrup

## Instructions

1. Preheat the oven to 400°F. Place a wire rack over a baking sheet.
2. Combine the plant milk, flour, aquafaba, maple syrup, cinnamon, and salt (if using) in a bowl and stir until the mixture is smooth. Transfer to a shallow pan. Stir in the orange zest and mix well.
3. Warm a nonstick skillet over medium heat. Dip each bread slice

into the mixture and let soak for a few seconds. Turn over and soak for a few seconds more. Place in the skillet and cook over medium-low heat for 2 to 3 minutes. Turn over gently, then cook the other side for 2 to 3 minutes, until golden brown.

4. Place the toast on the wire rack and bake in the oven for 10 to 15 minutes, until crisp.

5. Combine berries, applesauce, and maple syrup in a blender and pulse until sauce reaches a chunky consistency.

6. Serve the french toast warm with the berry compote.

- Chocolate Chip Coconut Pancakes

These pancakes are so simple and delicious, and they're just as good for dessert as they are for breakfast! Plus, they freeze really well, so you can make an extra batch and freeze them. Use a large griddle so that you can cook three or four at a time.

Total time: 30 min

Serves: 8

**Ingredients**

✓ 1 tablespoon flaxseeds

- ✓ 1¼ cups buckwheat flour
- ✓ ¼ cup old-fashioned rolled oats
- ✓ 2 tablespoons unsweetened coconut flakes
- ✓ 1 tablespoon baking powder
- ✓ Pinch of sea salt
- ✓ 1 cup unsweetened, unflavored plant milk
- ✓ ½ cup unsweetened applesauce
- ✓ ¼ cup pure maple syrup
- ✓ 1 teaspoon pure vanilla extract
- ✓ ⅓ cup grain-sweetened, vegan mini chocolate chips
- ✓ Sliced bananas, for serving

## Instructions

1. Place the flaxseeds in a small saucepan with ½ cup water. Cook over medium heat until the mixture gets a little sticky and

appears stringy when it drips off a spoon, 3 to 4 minutes. Immediately strain the mixture into a glass measuring cup and set aside. Discard the seeds.

2. In a large bowl, whisk together the buckwheat flour, oats, coconut flakes, baking powder, and salt.

3. In a medium bowl, whisk together the milk, applesauce, maple syrup, vanilla, and 2 tablespoons of the reserved flax water.

4. Add the liquid mixture to the dry mix and stir together to blend; the batter will be thick. Stir in the chocolate chips.

5. Heat a nonstick griddle over medium-low heat. Pour ⅓ cup batter for each pancake onto the griddle and spread gently. Cook

for 6 to 8 minutes, until the pancakes look slightly dry on top, are lightly browned on the bottom, and release easily from the pan. Flip and cook for about 5 minutes on the other side.

6. Repeat for the remaining batter, wiping off the griddle between batches. Serve hot with sliced bananas.

**Storage:** Place cooked pancakes in an airtight container and refrigerate for up to 5 days or frozen for up to 1 month. Reheat pancakes in a 350°F oven for 15 minutes for refrigerated pancakes and 25 minutes if frozen.

- Banana Almond Granola

This recipe was inspired by my favorite banana almond muffins. Whether in muffins or in cereal, bananas and almonds pair perfectly.

Total time: 75 min

Serves: 16

**Ingredients**

- ✓ 8 cups rolled oats
- ✓ 2 cups pitted and chopped dates
- ✓ 2 ripe bananas, peeled and chopped

- ✓ 1 teaspoon almond extract
- ✓ 1 teaspoon salt
- ✓ 1 cup slivered almonds, toasted (optional)

## Instructions

1. Preheat the oven to 275°F.
2. Add the oats to a large bowl and set aside. Line two 13 × 18-inch baking sheets with parchment paper.
3. Place the dates in a medium saucepan with 1 cup of water and bring to a boil. Cook over medium heat for 10 minutes. Add more water if needed to keep the dates from sticking to the pan.

4. Remove from the heat and add the mixture to a blender with the bananas, almond extract, and salt. Process until smooth and creamy.
5. Add the date mixture to the oats and mix well. Divide the granola between the two prepared baking sheets and spread out evenly.
6. Bake for 40 to 50 minutes, stirring every 10 minutes, until the granola is crispy. Remove from the oven and let cool before adding the slivered almonds (if using). (The cereal will get even crispier as it cools.)
7. Store the granola in an airtight container.

- Chickpea Omelet

This wonderful egg-free omelet is easy to make and is good for breakfast, lunch, or dinner.

Total time: 30 min

Serves: 3-6

**Ingredients**

- ✓ 1 cup chickpea flour
- ✓ ½ teaspoon onion powder
- ✓ ½ teaspoon garlic powder
- ✓ ¼ teaspoon white pepper
- ✓ ¼ teaspoon black pepper

- ✓ 1/3 cup nutritional yeast
- ✓ ½ teaspoon baking soda
- ✓ 3 green onions (white and green parts), chopped
- ✓ 4 ounces sautéed mushrooms (optional)

## Instructions

1. Combine the chickpea flour, onion powder, garlic powder, white pepper, black pepper, nutritional yeast, and baking soda in a small bowl. Add 1 cup water and stir until the batter is smooth.
2. Heat a frying pan over medium heat. Pour the batter into the pan, as if making pancakes. Sprinkle 1 to 2 tablespoons of the green

onions and mushrooms into the batter for each omelet as it cooks. Flip the omelet. When the underside is browned, flip the omelet again, and cook the other side for a minute.

3. Serve your amazing Chickpea Omelet topped with tomatoes, spinach, salsa, hot sauce, or whatever heart-safe, plant-perfect fixings you like.

- Polenta with Pears and Cranberries

This polenta recipe is one of my favorites! For this recipe use the ripest pears you can find on the market—Bosc, Asian, or D'anjou—and fresh cranberries when they are in season (usually from October through December).

Total time: 15 min

Serves: 4

**Ingredients**

- ✓ 1/4 cup brown rice syrup
- ✓ 2 pears, peeled, cored, and diced
- ✓ 1 cup fresh or dried cranberries
- ✓ 1 teaspoon ground cinnamon
- ✓ 1 batch Basic Polenta, kept warm

## Instructions

1. Heat the brown rice syrup in a medium saucepan. Add the pears, cranberries, and cinnamon and cook, stirring occasionally, until the pears are tender, about 10 minutes.
2. To serve, divide the polenta among 4 individual bowls and top with the pear compote.

- Fruit and Nut Oatmeal

Oatmeal is one of my favorite breakfast foods. It is quick to prepare and easily adaptable to my ever-changing moods—some days I want it with fruit, some days I want it plain, and sometimes I want a little bit of everything in it. This basic recipe is all you need to get started … add as much or as little of the extras as you like.

Total time: 15 min

Serves: 1

## Ingredients

- ✓ ¾ cup rolled oats
- ✓ ¼ teaspoon ground cinnamon
- ✓ Pinch of sea salt
- ✓ ¼ cup fresh berries (optional)
- ✓ ½ ripe banana, sliced (optional)
- ✓ 2 tablespoons chopped nuts, such as walnuts, pecans, or cashews (optional)
- ✓ 2 tablespoons dried fruit, such as raisins, cranberries, chopped apples, chopped
- ✓ Apricots (optional)
- ✓ Maple syrup (optional)

## Instructions

1. Combine the oats and 1½ cups water in a small saucepan. Bring

to a boil over high heat. Reduce the heat to medium-low and cook until the water has been absorbed, about 5 minutes.

2. Stir in the cinnamon and salt. Top with the berries, banana, nuts, and/or dried fruit, as you like. If desired, pour a little maple syrup on top. Serve hot.

- Egyptian Breakfast Beans

This traditional Egyptian breakfast (pronounced fool mudammis) is almost always made with dried fava beans. They need to soak at least 8 hours before cooking, so start this dish the day before you want to serve it, to let the beans soak overnight. Ful Medames is usually served with pita bread and a fried egg, but take some liberty and serve it over brown rice with fresh lemon instead.

Total time: 2 15min

Serves: 4

## Ingredients

- ✓ 1½ pounds dried fava beans, soaked for 8 to 10 hours
- ✓ 1 medium yellow onion, peeled and diced small
- ✓ 4 cloves garlic, peeled and minced
- ✓ 1 teaspoon ground cumin
- ✓ Zest and juice of 1 lemon
- ✓ Sea salt
- ✓ 1 lemon, quartered

## Instructions

1. Drain and rinse the beans and add them to a large pot. Cover with 4 inches of water and bring to a boil over high heat. Reduce the heat to

medium, cover, and cook until the beans are tender, 1½ to 2 hours.

2. While the beans are cooking, sauté the onion in a medium skillet or saucepan over medium heat for 8 to 10 minutes, or until it is tender and starting to brown. Add the garlic, cumin, and lemon zest and juice and cook for 5 minutes longer. Set aside.

3. When the beans are fully cooked, drain all but ½ cup of the liquid from the pot and add the onion mixture to the beans. Mix well and season with salt to taste. Serve garnished with the lemon quarters.

- Apple-Lemon Breakfast Bowl

Fresh and deliciously filling, this apple-lemon breakfast bowl is beautifully flavored with dates, cinnamon, and walnuts.

Total time: 15 min

Serves: 2

**Ingredients**

- ✓ 4 to 5 medium apples, any variety
- ✓ 5 to 6 dates, pitted
- ✓ Juice of 1 lemon (about 3 tablespoons)

✓ 2 tablespoons walnuts (about 6 walnut halves)
✓ ¼ teaspoon ground cinnamon

## Instructions

1. Core the apples and cut into large pieces.
2. Place dates, half of the lemon juice, walnuts, cinnamon, and three quarters of the apple in the bowl of a food processor. Puree until finely ground, scraping down the sides of the bowl as needed.
3. Add the remainder of the apples and lemon juice and pulse until the apples are shredded and the date mixture is evenly distributed.

- Breakfast Scramble

There are many very good recipes for scrambles, but most call for tofu. In this recipe, cauliflower takes the place of the tofu—with delicious results.

Total time: 30

Serves: 6

**Ingredients**

✓ 1 red onion, peeled and cut into ½-inch dice

- ✓ 1 red bell pepper, seeded and cut into ½-inch dice
- ✓ 1 green bell pepper, seeded and cut into ½-inch dice
- ✓ 2 cups sliced mushrooms (from about 8 ounces whole mushrooms)
- ✓ 1 large head cauliflower, cut into florets, or 2 (19-ounce) cans ackee, drained and gently rinsed
- ✓ Sea salt
- ✓ ½ teaspoon freshly ground black pepper
- ✓ 1½ teaspoons turmeric
- ✓ ¼ teaspoon cayenne pepper, or to taste
- ✓ 3 cloves garlic, peeled and minced
- ✓ 1 to 2 tablespoons low-sodium soy sauce
- ✓ ¼ cup nutritional yeast (optional)

## Instructions

1. Place the onion, red and green peppers, and mushrooms in a medium skillet or saucepan and sauté over medium-high heat for 7 to 8 minutes, or until the onion is translucent. Add water 1 to 2 tablespoons at a time to keep the vegetables from sticking to the pan.
2. Add the cauliflower and cook for 5 to 6 minutes, or until the florets are tender.
3. Add the salt to taste, pepper, turmeric, cayenne, garlic, soy sauce, and nutritional yeast (if using) to the pan, and cook for 5 minutes more, or until hot and fragrant.

- Brown Rice Breakfast Pudding

My mom used to serve a version of this for breakfast—cooked with milk, sugar, and a hint of cinnamon. It is still one of my favorite breakfasts, although now I make a more wholesome version with almond milk and chopped dates.

Total time: 15 min

Serves: 4

## Ingredients

- ✓ 3 cups cooked brown rice
- ✓ 2 cups unsweetened almond milk
- ✓ 1 cinnamon stick
- ✓ ⅛ to ¼ teaspoon ground cloves, to taste
- ✓ 1 cup dates, pitted and chopped
- ✓ 1 tart apple (such as Granny Smith), cored and chopped
- ✓ ¼ cup raisins
- ✓ Salt to taste
- ✓ ¼ cup slivered almonds, toasted

## Instructions

1. Combine the rice, almond milk, cinnamon stick, cloves, and dates in a medium saucepan and cook, stirring occasionally, over

medium-low heat for 12 minutes, or until the mixture thickens.

2. Remove the cinnamon stick. Add the apple, raisins, and salt and mix.

3. Serve garnished with the toasted almonds.

- Chocolate Pancakes

Everybody deserves to have a little chocolate for breakfast once in a while. These pancakes got five-star reviews from all of my testers. This recipe requires a nonstick skillet to keep the pancakes from sticking. Serve with whatever fresh fruit you like—we enjoy them with strawberries, raspberries, bananas, or a combination of all three.

Total time: 30 min

Serves: 12

# Ingredients

- ✓ 1¼ cups whole-grain gluten-free flour (see Notes)
- ✓ 2 tablespoons unsweetened cocoa powder
- ✓ 1 tablespoon baking powder
- ✓ 1 tablespoon ground flaxseed
- ✓ 1 tablespoon vegan mini chocolate chips (optional; see Notes)
- ✓ ¼ teaspoon sea salt
- ✓ 1 cup unsweetened, unflavored almond milk
- ✓ 1 tablespoon pure maple syrup or ¼ teaspoon stevia powder
- ✓ 1 teaspoon vanilla extract
- ✓ 1 tablespoon apple cider vinegar
- ✓ ¼ cup unsweetened applesauce

# Instructions

1. Combine the dry ingredients (flour, cocoa powder, baking powder, flax, chocolate chips, and salt) in a medium bowl. Whisk until fully combined.
2. Combine the wet ingredients (almond milk, maple syrup, vanilla, and vinegar) in a small bowl, and whisk well. This will create a vegan buttermilk for your pancakes.
3. Add the vegan buttermilk and the applesauce to the flour mixture, and stir until the batter is just combined.
4. Let the batter stand for 10 minutes while it rises and thickens as the flaxseeds soak; it may nearly double in size.

5. Heat a nonstick skillet or electric skillet griddle over medium heat and mist with a tiny bit of nonstick spray, if desired. (If you have a large skillet, you can cook multiple pancakes at once.) Scoop the batter into 3-inch rounds. Cook for 2 to 3 minutes or until the bubbles have burst in each of the pancakes and the tops start to appear dry. Flip the pancakes and cook for 1 to 2 minutes more. You should get 12 pancakes total.

**Notes**:

**Flour** - You can use any other whole-grain flour if you prefer.

**Chocolate chips** - Two brands of vegan mini chocolate chips I like are

Enjoy Life and Lily's (stevia-sweetened).

- Black Bean and Sweet Potato Hash

This black bean and sweet potato hash can be an ideal breakfast, a lunch, or a light dinner. It can be served simply as a side dish, spooned over brown rice or quinoa, wrapped in a whole-wheat tortilla, or made into soft tacos garnished with avocado, cilantro, and other favorite toppings. Make it in your Instant Pot or other pressure cooker, or do it the old-fashioned way, on the stovetop.

Total time: 30 min

Serves: 4

## Ingredients

- ✓ 1 cup chopped onion
- ✓ 1 to 2 cloves garlic, minced
- ✓ 2 cups chopped peeled sweet potatoes (about 2 small or medium)
- ✓ 2 teaspoons mild or hot chili powder
- ✓ ⅓ cup low-sodium vegetable broth
- ✓ 1 cup cooked black beans
- ✓ ¼ cup chopped scallions
- ✓ Splash of hot sauce (optional)
- ✓ Chopped cilantro, for garnish

## Instructions

Stovetop Method

1. Place the onions in a nonstick skillet and sauté over medium- heat, stirring

occasionally, for 2 to 3 minutes. Add the garlic and stir.

2. Add the sweet potatoes and chili powder, and stir to coat the vegetables with the chili powder. Add broth and stir. Cook for about 12 minutes more, stirring occasionally, until the potatoes are cooked through. Add more liquid 1 to 2 tablespoons at a time as needed, to keep the vegetables from sticking to the pan.

3. Add the black beans, scallions, and salt. Cook for 1 or 2 minutes more, until the beans are heated through.

4. Add the hot sauce (if using), and stir. Taste and adjust the seasonings. Top with chopped cilantro and serve.

Pressure Cooker Method

1. Heat a stovetop pressure cooker over medium heat or set an electric cooker to sauté. Add the onion and cook, stirring occasionally, for 2 to 3 minutes. Add the garlic and stir. Add the sweet potatoes and chili powder. Stir to coat the sweet potatoes with the chili powder. Add the broth and stir.

2. Lock the lid on the pressure cooker. Bring to high pressure for 3 minutes. Quick release the pressure. Remove the lid, tilting it away from you.

3. Add the black beans, scallions, and salt. Cook for 1 or 2 minutes more over medium heat, or lock on the lid for 3 minutes, until the beans are heated through.

4. Add the hot sauce (if using), and stir. Taste and adjust the seasonings. Top with chopped cilantro and serve.

- Easy Overnight Oats With Chia

To get through those busy weeks, try this easy and healthy breakfast that you can make the night before.

Total time: 8 hours

Serves: 1

## Ingredients

- ✓ ¾ cup gluten-free rolled oats
- ✓ ¼ cup plant milk
- ✓ ½ cup water
- ✓ 1 heaping tablespoon chia seeds
- ✓ ½-1 tablespoon maple syrup

- ✓ ¼ teaspoon cinnamon
- ✓ Dash of vanilla bean powder or extract
- ✓ Fruit of choice

## Instructions

1. Place oats, liquid, chia seeds, maple syrup, cinnamon, and vanilla into a 16-ounce mason jar or container of choice. Mix well. Seal shut and place jar in refrigerator overnight.
2. In the morning, mix again and top with anything you'd like, such as fresh fruit, more chia seeds, or cacao nibs.

- Whole-Wheat Berry Muffins

These are a perfectly delicious breakfast muffin with loads of berry goodness and a tasty, wheaty backdrop. If you can find wild blueberries, use them—they are perfect for muffins because they're tiny and distribute beautifully without making the muffin soggy.

Total time: 1 hour

Serves: 12

**Ingredients**

- ✓ ⅔ cup unsweetened plant-based milk
- ✓ 1 tablespoon ground flaxseeds
- ✓ 1 teaspoon apple cider vinegar
- ✓ 2 cups whole-wheat pastry flour
- ✓ 2 teaspoons baking powder
- ✓ ¼ teaspoon baking soda
- ✓ ¾ teaspoon salt
- ✓ ½ cup unsweetened applesauce
- ✓ ½ cup pure maple syrup
- ✓ 1½ teaspoons pure vanilla extract
- ✓ 1 cup berries

## Instructions

1. Preheat the oven to 350°F. Line a 12-cup muffin pan with silicone liners or use a nonstick or silicone muffin pan.
2. In a large measuring cup, use a fork to vigorously mix together

the plant-based milk, flaxseeds, and vinegar. Mix for about a minute, until it appears foamy. Set aside.

3. In a medium mixing bowl, sift together the flour, baking powder, baking soda, and salt. Make a well in the center and pour in the milk mixture. Add the applesauce, maple syrup, and vanilla to the well and stir together. Incorporate the dry ingredients into the wet ingredients until the dry ingredients are moistened (do not overmix). Fold in the berries.

4. Fill each muffin cup three-quarters full and bake for 22 to 26 minutes, or until a knife inserted through the center of a muffin comes out clean.

5. Let the muffins cool completely, about 20 minutes, then carefully run a knife around the edges of each muffin to remove them from the pan.

- Apple-Walnut Breakfast Bread

Slightly sweet, oil-free, and totally satisfying, this makes a great breakfast on the run. I know you want to eat it all in one sitting (I do, too), so to avoid that calorie splurge, cut it into single servings, wrap each in plastic wrap, and put them in the freezer until needed. This also makes a great baked gift.

Wrap it up, tie it with a bow—now you're everyone's favorite breakfast baker!

Total time: 60 min

Serves: 8

## Ingredients

- ✓ 1½ cups unsweetened applesauce
- ✓ ¾ cup packed light brown sugar
- ✓ ⅓ cup plain unsweetened almond milk or plant milk
- ✓ 1 tablespoon ground flax seeds mixed with 2 tablespoons warm water
- ✓ 2 cups all-purpose or whole wheat flour
- ✓ 1 teaspoon baking soda
- ✓ ½ teaspoon baking powder
- ✓ 1 teaspoon salt

✓ 1 teaspoon ground cinnamon

✓ ½ cup chopped walnuts

## Instructions

1. Preheat the oven to 375°F.

2. In a large bowl, combine the applesauce, brown sugar, almond milk, and flax mixture and stir until smooth and well mixed. Set aside.

3. In a separate bowl, combine the flour, baking soda, baking powder, salt, and cinnamon. Mix the dry ingredients into the wet ingredients just until blended. Stir in the walnuts, then transfer the batter to a 9x5-inch loaf pan, spreading evenly and smoothing the top.

4. Bake until golden brown and a toothpick inserted in the center comes out clean, 25 to 30 minutes. Cool in the pan for about 20 minutes, then remove from the pan and cool completely on a wire rack.

# LUNCH

- Mediterranean Pinwheels

These Mediterranean Pinwheels are a super easy and ultimately delicious snack and party food. Made with tomatoes, artichokes, and olives, they get their awesome flavor kick by the homemade Tahini sauce. All vegan and gluten free.

Total time: 6 min

Serves: 16

**Ingredients**

# FOR THE TAHINI SAUCE:

- ✓ 3 Tbs Tahini Paste
- ✓ 3 Tbs Lemon juice
- ✓ 4 Tbs white vinegar
- ✓ 1/2 cup (120 ml) water
- ✓ 1 glove garlic
- ✓ salt pepper to taste
- ✓ FOR THE PINWHEELS:
- ✓ olives
- ✓ cherry tomatoes
- ✓ artichokes in a jar
- ✓ lettuce
- ✓ tortillas, gluten-free

**Instructions**

FOR THE TAHINI SAUCE:

1. Whisk together all ingredients in a small bowl until the sauce is creamy.

## TO ASSEMBLE THE PINWHEELS:

2. Cut the tomatoes, artichokes, and olives into slices.
3. Spread about one Tbs of the Tahini sauce on one tortilla. Add the vegetables and top with a handful of salad.
4. Tightly roll the tortillas and cut into pinwheels.

• Mint Chocolate Truffle

These homemade Larabar Bites can be made in minutes and are full of wholesome plant-based ingredients. They taste like chewy mint chocolate brownies & are perfect for satisfying your sweet cravings!

Larabars are great but they aren't cheap and they are so easy to make yourself. I spotted the new Mint Chocolate Truffle Larabar Bites recently and they look awesome. They are a little bit more decadent than regular Larabars and are more truffle-like, but they are pretty expensive for the amount you get in the bag. I knew that I could probably whip some Homemade Larabar Bites myself and they would be much more budget friendly.

## Ingredients

- ✓ 130g | 10 large medjool dates , pitted
- ✓ 200g | 1½ cups raw almonds
- ✓ 180g | 1 cup chocolate chips , I used semi-sweet dark ones
- ✓ 20g | ¼ cup cocoa powder
- ✓ 28g | ¼ cup coconut flour
- ✓ ¼ - ½ teaspoon peppermint extract , or 5 - 10 drops peppermint oil, (start at the lower end of the scale then taste once it's mixed together. If you would prefer it a little

stronger then add some more but do it very gradually)

✓ 2 tablespoons water

## Instructions

1. Put the almonds in a food processor and blend until a fine flour.
2. Add the dates, chocolate chips, coconut flour and cocoa and process again until well combined.
3. Add the peppermint extract/oil and water.
4. Process until well combined and balling up.
5. Taste a tiny bit and add more peppermint if required. Process again to combine if you do,

6. Remove the blade and form the dough into balls. You can make them whatever size you prefer. Mine were the size of walnuts.
7. Notes
8. Store in an airtight container in the fridge. They will keep for up to 3 weeks.

- Veggie Wrap With Apples And Spicy Hummus

This Veggie Wrap is loaded with healthy veggies, crunchy apples, and a spicy hummus for kick. It makes a super quick and easy lunch!

Total time: 10 min

Serves: 1

## Ingredients

- ✓ 1 tortilla (your favorite) (gluten free, if desired)
- ✓ 3-4 tbsp Spicy Hummus (or use your favorite store bought hummus and mix it with a few tbsp of salsa)
- ✓ A few leaves of romaine lettuce or fresh spinach (or the leafy green of your choice)

- ✓ 1/2 cup broccoli slaw
- ✓ 1/4 apple (sliced thin)
- ✓ 2 tsp dairy free plain unsweetened yogurt
- ✓ 1/2 tsp fresh lemon juice
- ✓ salt & pepper (to taste)

## Instructions

1. Mix the yogurt and lemon juice with the broccoli slaw. Add a dash of salt and pepper, to taste, and mix well. Set aside.
2. Lay tortilla flat.
3. Spread spicy hummus all over the tortilla.
4. Lay down the lettuce on top of the spicy hummus.

5. On one half, pile the broccoli slaw over the lettuce.
6. Place the apple slices on top of the slaw.
7. Fold up the sides of the tortilla and then, starting with the end that has the slaw and apples, roll tightly.
8. Cut in half and enjoy!

## Recipe Notes

~The Spicy Hummus can be made ahead of time and will keep in the fridge for several days.

- Jamaican jerk tofu wrap

How can it already be time to get the kids, or yourself, ready to go back to school? In my neck of the woods, summer weather just arrived, it just doesn't seem fair. Unfortunately, it is what it is, so instead of whining, just wine, because that always makes things better. Another thing that makes going back to school, or work, better is being armed with an arsenal of easy and healthy vegan lunch ideas. In this section am going top show you a yummy menu that will make you and the kids look forward to brown bagging it, beginning with this rockin' Jamaican Jerk Tofu wrap.

Total time: 1hr 15min

Serves: 2

## Ingredients

- ✓ 14 oz tofu Sliced into 1/2 inch long pieces
- ✓ Marinade
- ✓ 1/4 cup of Soy Sauce
- ✓ 2 tablespoons of apple cider vinegar
- ✓ 1 tablespoon of tomato paste
- ✓ 2 teaspoons of maple syrup
- ✓ 1 teaspoon of ground black pepper add more if you like it spicier
- ✓ 1 and 1/2 teaspoons of ground sea salt

- ✓ 2 teaspoons of nutmeg
- ✓ 2 teaspoons of cinnamon
- ✓ 2 teaspoons of allspice
- ✓ 2 cloves of garlic – minced
- ✓ 1 small scotch bonnet pepper – seeded and minced
- ✓ 1 teaspoon of avocado oil to coat the pan for cooking optional if you have a non-stick pan
- ✓ For the Wrap
- ✓ 2 whole grain tortillas
- ✓ 2 cups of baby spinach leaves
- ✓ 1 yellow bell pepper – seeded and cut into strips
- ✓ 1 small tomato – seeded and finely diced
- ✓ 4 to 5 strips of Jamaican jerk tofu
- ✓ Sriracha or your favorite condiment optional

**Instructions**

For the tofu:

1. Cut it into thin slices (approximately 1/2 inch thick) and press them between paper towels. Put something heavy on top of the top layer of towels and keep changing the towels as they become soaked with water. Do this for about 10 minutes, or until the tofu feels drier.

For the marinade:

- In a large shallow bowl, add the marinade ingredients and whisk together until fully combined. Put the tofu in the marinade. Turn the tofu a few times to cover both sides in the marinade. Marinated for 1 hour (turn the tofu after 30 minutes).

To cook:

2. Heat a large skillet on medium-high heat and cover with a thin layer of avocado oil. You need the oil or the tofu will stick because of the maple syrup that's in the marinade. When the pan is hot, place the tofu in the pan and cook for approximately 5 to 8 minutes. It will turn a beautiful caramelized color. Now gently flip to the other side and cook for another 5 to 8 minutes.

For the Wrap:

3. Put one cup of spinach on a tortilla, then half of the bell pepper strips, half of the diced tomato, and 4 to 5 strips of jerk tofu. Drizzle with sriracha or your favorite condiment if you like. Wrap tightly and cut in half.

- Raw Vegan Collard Wraps

Raw vegan recipes are perfect when you want to eat healthy and detox your body from heavy meals or processed food. These collard wraps are going to be your new favorite healthy lunch. Ready in minutes and bursting with flavors from the avocados, red pepper, alfalfa, pecans and tamari mix. Gluten Free & Paleo too.

Total time: 15 min

Serves: 4

**Ingredients**

- ✓ 4 large collard leaves
- ✓ 1 red bell pepper
- ✓ 1 avocado
- ✓ 2-3 ounces alfalfa sprouts
- ✓ 1/2 lime
- ✓ 1 cup raw pecans
- ✓ 1 tablespoon tamari use coconut aminos for paleo version
- ✓ 1/2 teaspoon minced garlic
- ✓ 1/2 teaspoon grated ginger
- ✓ 1 teaspoon extra virgin olive oil

## Instructions

1. To prepare collard leaves wash leaves, cut off white stem at the bottom that has no leaves and place them in a bath of warm water with juice of half a lemon.

Let soak for 10 minutes. Dry the leaves off with paper towels and using a knife thinly slice down the central root (to make it easier to bend the leaves for wrapping).

2. Slice avocado and pepper.
3. In a food processor combine pecans, tamari, cumin (or garlic ginger mix) and olive oil. Pulse until combined and mixture clumps together.
4. Place a collard leaf in front of you and layer nut mix, red pepper slices, avocado slices, a drizzle of lime juice and alfalfa sprouts. Fold over the top and bottom and then wrap up the sides. Slice in half and serve.

- Rice paper rolls with mango and mint

Homemade rice paper rolls make such an awesome light dinner on hot summer days. They're healthy, low in calories, and super easy to make! Plus, they're also a wonderful appetizer for parties. I mean just look at that color!

These vegan rice paper rolls with mango, mint, and avocado with an easy peanut dipping sauce are just perfect for hot summer days.

**Ingredients**

For the rice paper rolls:

- ✓ 6 sheets Vietnamese rice paper
- ✓ 1 avocado
- ✓ 1 cucumber
- ✓ 3 small carrots
- ✓ 1 mango
- ✓ 3 green onions, cut into rings
- ✓ 1 cup purple cabbage, cut into thin stripes
- ✓ about 6 radishes, cut into thin slices
- ✓ 1 cup fresh mint
- ✓ 2-3 cups lettuce, cut into thin stripes
- ✓ 1 - 1 1/2 cups cooked glass noodles
- ✓ For the fried sesame tofu (optional):
- ✓ 7 oz block firm tofu

- ✓ 1 teaspoon sesame oil
- ✓ 1 tablespoon soy sauce
- ✓ 1 tablespoon sesame seeds
- ✓ For the peanut dipping sauce:
- ✓ 1/4 cup chunky peanut butter
- ✓ 2 teaspoons soy sauce
- ✓ 1 clove of garlic, minced
- ✓ 3-4 tablespoons warm water
- ✓ 1/2 teaspoons sriracha sauce (optional)

## Instructions

1. Cut the avocado, the carrots, the mango, the lettuce, and the purple cabbage into thing stripes.
2. When you're done cutting the veggies, fill a shallow bowl with water and dip the rice papers in water so they get moderately wet

on both sides. Don't let them soak too long, so they don't get too soft.

3. First make the tofu (it's optional but really yummy): Cut the tofu into thin stripes (about 0.10 inches thick) and heat the sesame oil in a medium-sized pan. Add the tofu and the soy sauce and cook for about 4 minutes until the tofu is brown and crispy. Then add the sesame seeds and cook for another minute.

4. When you soaked the rice papers, fill them with the veggies and the tofu (if using) and wrap them like a burrito. I think it's best to center the filling and then roll it up and fold in the two side flaps.

5. Then make the peanut dipping sauce: In a medium bowl, combine

the peanut butter with the soy sauce, the garlic, the warm water, and the sriracha sauce.

6. Serve the rice paper rolls with the peanut dipping sauce.

- Pita Pockets with Roasted Veggies and Hummus

Pita Pockets with Roasted Veggies and Hummus Recipe: Healthy and delicious lunch meal you will look forward to. These vegan rainbow pita pockets are very easy and quick to make and can be eaten warm or cold.

Total time: 1 hour

Serves: 1

**Ingredients**

For the pita pockets:

- ✓ 1 eggplant
- ✓ 2 carrots
- ✓ 1 red bell pepper
- ✓ 1 teaspoon Ras-el-Hanout
- ✓ 1 teaspoon turmeric
- ✓ 1/2 teaspoon sweet paprika
- ✓ 1/4 teaspoon freshly ground black pepper
- ✓ 1/4 teaspoon sea salt
- ✓ 4 loaves pita bread preferably whole grain
- ✓ 1 cup or 160 grams good quality store-bought or homemade hummus for homemade hummus, see the ingredient list below
- ✓ a handful baby spinach
- ✓ pomegranate seeds, to garnish
- ✓ chopped parsley, to garnish

For the hummus:

- ✓ 1 cup or 160 g chickpeas
- ✓ juice of 1/2 lemon
- ✓ 1 1/2 tablespoons tahini paste
- ✓ 1 small garlic clove
- ✓ 3 tablespoons extra virgin olive oil
- ✓ 1/2 teaspoon ground cumin
- ✓ 1/2 teaspoon Ras-el-Hanout (optional)
- ✓ 1/2 teaspoon turmeric (optional)
- ✓ 1/4 teaspoon sweet paprika (optional)
- ✓ a dash of chili flakes (optional)
- ✓ 2 tablespoons water start by adding 1 tablespoon, then continue adding 1 tablespoon at a time until desired consistency
- ✓ salt and freshly ground black pepper to taste

## Instructions

1. Preheat the oven to 200 °C or 400 °F. Julienne zour veggies: Cut the eggplant, carrots and bell peppers in 10 cm (4 inches) long strips and arrange them on a baking tray spayed with cooking spray. Sprinkle with spices (better combine them together in a small bowl), salt and black pepper and roast for about 25 minutes or until eggplant is tender.

2. Meanwhile, make the hummus if you want to make it yourself. Combine all the ingredients except water and blend until smoooth. Add water, 1 tablespoon at a time, until desired consistency.

3. Bake pita breads as per instruction on the package and cut them in halves. They will form pockets, so you can stuff them with about 2 tablespoons hummus each, a few strips of roasted veggies and a few leaves of baby spinach.

4. Lastly, sprinkle your pita pockets with pomegranate seeds and chopped parsley. If you don't follow a vegan diet, it's nice to drizzle them with a bit of Greek yogurt. Enjoy!

5. Recipe Notes

6. A small hack: if your kid wouldn't eat eggplants, sneak them into hummus!

7. You can adjust it to your taste or depending on what you have in your fridge.

- Blueberry coconut bliss balls

How about some velvety blueberry cake bites for a change of pace? ? I can't even begin to tell you how simple, yet comforting these little blueberry bliss balls are. Honestly, if you've ever had a Need-To-Satisfy-A-Cake-Craving-Right-Now situation on you hands, but without the time to mess with an oven… these will be your friend. What could be better than an instant cake-type fix which requires no baking and doesn't leave a massive amount of leftovers to test your willpower.

This recipe is extremely forgiving... nothing complicated about it, and best of all it's fast. You can go from dessert hankering to blueberry cake bliss in just 15 minutes. These are also perfect to take for snacks on the go or mid-day munchies.

Once you've processed the batter, make sure you roll it into balls straight away, otherwise if it sits around for too long, the coconut in the recipe (which is extremely absorbent) will cause it to dry out. If you find your batter is dry just add a touch more milk to bring it back to the right consistency before rolling.

Total time: 15 min

Serves: 14

## Ingredients

- ✓ 1 cup blueberry jam (can use this homemade recipe or a fruit-sweetened version (like St. Dalfour, which is what I used this time)
- ✓ 1¼ cup coconut flour
- ✓ ¼ cup maple syrup
- ✓ ¼ cup unsweetened plant milk (I used almond milk or can use a nut-free milk of your choice)
- ✓ ¼ tsp salt
- ✓ ½ cup shredded unsweetened coconut for rolling

## Instructions

1. Process all ingredients, except shredded coconut, in a food processor into a uniform mixture. Allow it to sit for a minute. Meanwhile spread the shredded coconut on a plate.
2. Use a 1 tbsp cookie scoop or just pick out even amounts of the dough with your hands and roll the mixture into balls. Roll each ball in the shredded coconut and set aside. Let them rest a few minutes and enjoy fresh or chilled! (I liked mine refrigerated).

- Grilled Green Goddess Wraps

No more boring lunches! These Grilled Green Goddess Wraps are full of green goodness and nutrition with a lima bean spread, broccoli, and hearts of palm! Gluten-free, nut-free, and vegan, these wraps are a healthy recipe that's school or work friendly and freezable!

Total time: 4 min

Serves: 2

**Ingredients**

Lima Bean Spread:

- ✓ 1 Cup Cooked Baby Lima Beans
- ✓ 2 TB Nutritional Yeast
- ✓ 2 TB Chopped Parsley
- ✓ ½ Tsp Minced Garlic
- ✓ ½ Tsp Onion Powder
- ✓ 2 Tsp Fresh Lime Juice
- ✓ 2 Tsp White Balsamic Vinegar

Wraps:

- ✓ 2 Large Gluten-free Vegan Wraps
- ✓ 1 Cup Raw Broccoli (sliced lengthwise)
- ✓ 2 Whole Hearts of Palm (sliced lengthwise)

## Instructions

1. In a food processor, blend together all the lima bean spread

ingredients until you get a thick hummus texture.

2. Take one wrap and lay it out flat. Spread ⅓ cup (half the lima bean spread) on ⅔s of the wrap. Then take about half the raw sliced broccoli and layer that on top of the spread. Take on of the sliced whole hearts of palm and so the same.

3. Roll the wrap like a burrito, tucking in the ends.

4. Heat a grill pan over high heat and grill the wrap, seam side down first, for about 2 minutes. Flip the wrap over and grill the other side for another 2 minutes.

5. Repeat this process for the other wrap(s).

6.

- Vegan Guacamole Stuffed Rolls

Close your eyes if you are looking for an extra healthy recipe, because these delicious savoury puff pastry rolls filled with a creamy and spicy avocado, zucchini and cashew cream are clearly not that type. These guacamole stuffed rolls are extra indulgent and probably not very diet friendly, but I'm sure you'll love these a lot still.

Guacamole stuffed rolls (or horns) are super simple to make and they are totally customisable – stuff them with hummus, your favourite vegan cream cheese, pesto or garlicky spinach, if you are not into guac. They make a great party snack, picnic food or grab-and-go lunch, though they are also lovely as a quick dinner with a big green salad.

Total time: 35 min

Serves: 8

**Ingredients**

- ✓ 1 sheet of puff pastry (make sure it's vegan)
- ✓ 2 tbsp plant milk
- ✓ 1 pinch turmeric
- ✓ For the filling:
- ✓ ⅔ cup cashews, soaked
- ✓ 1 zucchini

- ✓ 1 avocado
- ✓ 2 cloves of garlic
- ✓ 1 lemon, juice
- ✓ 1 tsp fresh, chopped chili pepper
- ✓ 1 tbsp chopped chives
- ✓ 2 scallions
- ✓ salt, pepper

## Instructions

1. Cut puff pastry into 8 strips and roll each strip on a roll or cream horn mold*, following the shape of the molds. Mix together milk and turmeric and brush the rolls with this mixture, so they get a nice, yellow colour.
2. Bake puff pastry rolls at 200°C/400°F for 20-25 minutes.

Cool completely, then remove the molds.

3. Meanwhile add cashews, diced zucchini, garlic and lemon juice to a food processor or blender, and processor until completely smooth. This might take a few minutes, so be patient. Once the mixture is smooth and creamy, add diced avocado, chopped chili pepper, chives and scallion, season with salt and pepper, and pulse a few times.

4. Pour the mixture into a piping bag and pipe the mixture into the puff pastry rolls. You can also dip the edges into chives, chili, lemon zest or some vegan cheese. Enjoy!

## NOTES

*If you don't have a store-bought roll or horn mold, you can make those easily at home too. Just take 2 empty tin foil rolls (the thin roll with very thick paper would work best), and wet them a bit. Then cut them into 4 pieces each and tightly wrap them in tin foil. You might need to brush these 'molds' with oil, so the rolls are easier to remove.

- Healthy Make-Ahead Burritos

Healthy make ahead bean and rice burritos are perfect for easy packed lunches. Find out how meal prep and freeze burritos. These burritos are vegetarian, vegan, and easy to make gluten-free. They have a hearty plant-based complete protein base to which you can add any veggies you like. Just don't forget to pack the guacamole!

**Ingredients**

✓ 6 warm tortillas (gluten free if needed)

- ✓ 2 (16 oz.) cans fat free refried beans
- ✓ 2 cups cooked rice or quinoa
- ✓ 1/2 cup mild salsa
- ✓ 1 tablespoon extra virgin olive oil
- ✓ any veggies you would like to add
- ✓ guacamole for serving

## Instructions

1. Preheat the oven to 375 degrees F. Transfer beans to a saucepan and warm to soften.
2. Place tortillas on a work surface. Spoon beans into a "log" just off center closest to your body. Be sure to leave about two inches on either side of the log. Top with rice and salsa. Add any vegetables you would like. Don't add avocado or guacamole. Starting from the

edge closest to you, tightly wrap the tortilla just over the fillings to seal. Tuck the sides in and continue rolling, as shown in the video. Place burrito on a cooking sheet. Continue until all the tortillas have been used. Brush the top and sides of burritos with olive oil. Bake for 15 minutes, or until light golden.

3. To store burritos for later, allow them to cool completely. Then transfer to a freezer bag or container. Freeze or refrigerate until ready to pack or eat. Reheat in the oven at 375 degrees for about 25 minutes oven or microwave for about 1 1/2 minutes.

- Smashed Chickpea Salad Bites

Tangy vegan smashed chickpea salad with mustard, pickles and chives is extremely delicious on these sweet and spicy bread bites made with rye bread, raisins and balsamic vinegar. I know, the internet is full with smashed chickpea salad recipes, but I couldn't resist to post my version too. It's such a simple and flavourful recipe, no wonder that everybody loves it. These bites make a great appetiser, barbecue side or picnic food. You can also eat this smashed chickpea salad in a good ol' sandwich or stuffed in potatoes.

Total time: 20 min

Serves: 10

**Ingredients**

For the bread

- ✓ 4 slices/1.5 cups of crumbled whole grain rye bread (I used pumpernickel)
- ✓ ⅓ cup of raisins or chopped dates
- ✓ 1 small chilli pepper (optional)
- ✓ 2 tbsp chopped fresh parsley
- ✓ 2 tbsp balsamic vinegar
- ✓ ½ tbsp maple syrup
- ✓ 1 tsp garlic powder
- ✓ ½ tsp smoked paprika
- ✓ ½ tsp cayenne pepper
- ✓ salt, pepper

For the salad

- ✓ 1 can of chickpeas
- ✓ 2 scallions
- ✓ ⅓ cup of chopped pickles
- ✓ ⅓ cup of soy or coconut yogurt
- ✓ 1 tsp mustard
- ✓ 1 clove of garlic
- ✓ 1 lemon, juice
- ✓ 1 tbsp poppy seeds
- ✓ 2 tbsp chopped fresh chives
- ✓ salt, pepper

## Instructions

Bread

1. Add crumbled bread, raisins, deseeded chilli pepper, parsley, vinegar, maple syrup and spices to a food processor and pulse until

just combined. You do not want to over-mix the mixture.

2. Use a small round cookie cutter (6 cm/2.3 inch) to form the bites. Take about 2 tablespoons of the mixture and gently press into the mold. Make sure the bites are not too thin, so they won't break (1 cm/0.5 inch is a good height). Repeat with the rest of the bread mixture.

Salad

1. Drain and rinse chickpeas, and add to a large bowl. Chop scallions, pickles and chives, and mince garlic.

2. Using a potato masher or a fork, mash chickpeas until chunky.

3. Add scallions, pickles, yogurt, mustard, garlic and lemon juice to chickpeas, season with salt and pepper and mix well.

Assembly

1. Top each bread bite with a large spoonful of smashed chickpea salad. Sprinkle with poppy seeds and chives. Enjoy!

- Vegan Basil Ricotta Pinwheels

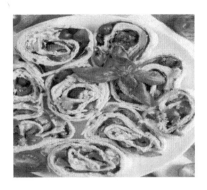

Some time ago, we had some friends over and I made these vegan basil ricotta pinwheels with fresh tomatoes, spinach, and olives. Let me tell you, they were gone super fast! So I guess it's save to say that they're a real crowd pleaser, not only among vegans but also meat-eaters. As they can be prepared in advance, they're perfect for parties or family get-togethers and also make for an easy and healthy lunch. I've always loved Mexican wraps, but this Mediterranean version really got me! And it definitely couldn't be easier!

Total time: 15 min

Serves: 4

**Ingredients**

For the basil ricotta cheese:

- ✓ 1/2 cup soaked unsalted cashews Soak them for about 30 minutes. If you have a heavy duty blender it also works without soaking.
- ✓ 1/4 cup almond milk
- ✓ 7 oz firm tofu (1 block)
- ✓ 1 teaspoon white wine vinegar
- ✓ about 20-25 fresh basil leaves
- ✓ 1 small clove of garlic
- ✓ salt
- ✓ pepper

For the wraps:

- ✓ 8 corn flour tortillas
- ✓ About 7 oz fresh spinach
- ✓ 2-3 tomatoes, chopped into small pieces
- ✓ 1/2 cup black olives, cut into rings

## Instructions

2. First make the basil ricotta cheese: Place all ingredients in a food processor and process until smooth.
3. Divide the basil ricotta evenly on the tortillas. Top with fresh spinach, chopped tomatoes, and black olives.
4. Tightly roll up the tortillas. Press edges to seal. Trim off the ends and cut each roll into 6-8 slices.

- Vegan Coconut Blueberry Muffins

Blueberries. Another reason to love this time of year. You can find blueberry everything, everywhere. I love it!

If you like those gigantic coffee shop muffins, you're gonna love these Vegan Coconut Blueberry Muffins! Lighter, satisfying and made with clean ingredients (and much smaller, too!)

Total time: 30 min

Serves: 12

**Ingredients**

- ✓ 1 flax egg (1 tbsp ground flax seeds mixed with 3 tbsp water) or one regular egg, if vegetarian.
- ✓ 1 ¾ cups whole wheat pastry flour
- ✓ ¾ cup unsweetened shredded coconut
- ✓ 2 ½ tsp baking powder
- ✓ ½ tsp salt
- ✓ ¾ cup coconut oil, softened
- ✓ ½ cup maple syrup or agave nectar
- ✓ ¼ cup sugar
- ✓ ¾ cup unsweetened non dairy milk, lukewarm ( see note 1)
- ✓ 1 to 1 1/2 cups blueberries (fresh or frozen)
- ✓ Cooking spray

## Instructions

1. Preheat the oven at 400F. Line a muffin pan with 12 liners and coat them with cooking spray
2. Combine the ground flax seeds with 3 tbsp water In a small bowl. Set aside
3. Combine the flour, shredded coconut, baking powder and salt in a medium bowl and set aside
4. Using an electric mixer, beat the coconut oil, maple syrup or agave and sugar together at medium speed until creamy, 2-3 minutes. Add the milk and flax mixture and keep beating until well combined (the mixture might look curdled)
5. Add the flour mixture and beat at low speed until just combined (do not overmix). Gently fold in the

blueberries using a wooden spoon or a spatula

6. Scoop about 1/4 cup of batter into the muffin liners (we like using an ice cream scoop or a cup measuring cup to make sure they are all the same size). Bake for 25-30 minutes

**NOTES**

Make sure the the non dairy milk is lukewarm. Other wise cold milk can make the coconut oil harden and it will be hard to mix.

- Greek Zoodle Bowl

This Greek Zoodle Bowl is a simple, easy summer meal that is ready in minutes, full of flavor and packed with veggies! Vegan, paleo, whole30, gluten free, grain free and delicious!

This Greek Zoodle Bowl would be the perfect lunch, as the zoodles won't wilt like traditional lettuce does in your favorite Greek Salad. Yes that means you can make this the night before, dressing and all, and enjoy it the next day for lunch, without wilty lettuce.

The cucumbers and zucchini will give off a little water but that will be at the bottom of the bowl mixing with the dressing, so that won't be a problem at all.

Total time: 10 min

Serves: 2

**Ingredients**

- ✓ 2 zucchini spiralized
- ✓ 1/2 English cucumber spiralized
- ✓ 1/2 red bell pepper chopped
- ✓ 1/2 yellow bell pepper chopped
- ✓ 6-7 cherry tomatoes chopped
- ✓ 2-3 tbs. chopped red onion
- ✓ 1/4 cup jarred artichokes chopped
- ✓ few sprigs of parsley chopped
- ✓ 1 sprig of mint leaves removed, chopped

✓ 3 tbs. hemp hearts

Greek Dressing

✓ 1/2 tsp. garlic powder
✓ 1 tsp. italian seasoning with oregano I used Fronteir Brand
✓ 1/4 tsp. salt
✓ 1 1/2 tbs. red wine vinegar
✓ 1/2 tbs. olive oil
✓ 1 sprig mint leaves removed, chopped

## Instructions

Salad

1. Spiralize the zucchini and cucumber and divide in two bowls
2. Chop the veggies and herbs, divide between the two bowls
3. Add the hemp hearts and anything else you want to add for protein

## Greek Dressing

1. Make the dressing in a small container with a tight fitting lid.
2. Add the seasoning, red wine vinegar, olive oil and chopped mint. Shake well.
3. Pour dressing over the salad, enjoy!
4.

## DINNER

Before you start imagining yourself on an austerity diet of bland blocks of tofu and big bowls of salad for dinner every night, let us reassure you: plant-based recipes are creative, mouth-watering, and generally amazing.

Here are some of my favorite plant-based dinners.

- Root Vegetable And Red Bean Stew

This recipe was created because I had a bunch of root vegetables and nothing really for the main course, so I decided to make them the main course. Add some beans in the mix and you have yourself a stew!

Served on top of rice, this is a hearty, satisfying meal and the flavor was fantastic. I hope you make it soon!

Serves: 6

**ingredients**

- ✓ 2 teaspoons extra virgin olive oil
- ✓ 1 onion, chopped
- ✓ 2 carrots, peeled and sliced into 1″ chunks
- ✓ 1 turnip, peeled and cut into 1″ chunks

- ✓ 1 rutabaga, peeled and cut into 1″ chunks
- ✓ 1 sweet potato, peeled and cut into 1 " chunks
- ✓ 1 1/2 cups vegetable stock
- ✓ 1 (14.5 ounce) can diced tomatoes, drained
- ✓ 2 (15 ounce) cans kidney beans, drained and rinsed
- ✓ 2 teaspoons coriander
- ✓ 1 teaspoons turmeric
- ✓ 1/2 teaspoon ground ginger
- ✓ pinch cinnamon
- ✓ sea salt and freshly ground black pepper
- ✓ Optional for serving: rice and sharp cheddar cheese (dairy or non-dairy variety to keep this vegan)

## instructions

1. In a medium pot, heat olive oil over medium heat. Add onion and sauté until soft and starting to brown, about 5-8 minutes.
2. Add the carrots, rutabaga, turnip, sweet potato, vegetable broth, coriander, turmeric, and ginger and bring to a boil. Reduce heat and simmer, uncovered, until the vegetables are fork tender, about 20 minutes.
3. Stir in the tomatoes, beans, and cinnamon and cook 2-3 more minutes. Add salt and pepper to taste.
4. Serve on top of brown rice and top with shredded sharp cheddar cheese, if desired. Enjoy!

- vegetable pumpkin curry

If there's one dinner idea I never get sick of, it's anything with curry. Give me some vegetables and a curry-flavored sauce, and I'm in dinner heaven.

HOWEVER. Lately, he's been tolerating it more than usual. I think his taste preferences are expanding! I'm celebrating over here!

Total time: 30 min

Serves: 4

## Ingredients

- ✓ 1 tablespoon avocado oil
- ✓ 1 large yellow onion, chopped
- ✓ 1/2 green cabbage, chopped
- ✓ 2 cups cauliflower pieces, chopped
- ✓ 2 cups small pieces broccoli florets
- ✓ for the pumpkin curry sauce
- ✓ 1 (15 ounce) can pumpkin puree
- ✓ 1 (15 ounce) can coconut milk (I prefer full fat, but lite should be fine)
- ✓ 1/2 cup water
- ✓ 2 tablespoons curry powder*
- ✓ 1 teaspoon ground ginger
- ✓ 1/2 teaspoon salt
- ✓ 1/4 teaspoon pepper

## Instructions

1. Heat the avocado oil in a large skillet. Add the onion and cabbage and cook until softened, about 5 minutes.
2. Add the cauliflower and cook another 5 minutes.
3. Add the broccoli and season all the vegetables with a little salt and pepper. Continue to cook another 4-5 minutes.
4. Meanwhile, in a medium bowl, whisk together the pumpkin, coconut milk, curry powder, ground ginger, salt and pepper.
5. Add the sauce to the pan of vegetables and stir to combine. Bring the mixture to a simmer and simmer until the sauce thickens slightly, about 5 more minutes.

Serve over rice, cauliflower rice, or alone. Enjoy!

**notes**

* I use a mild curry. If you use a spicy curry, you may want to adjust the amount you use based on your preferences.

- roasted portobello fajitas

One of the most frequent questions I get is, "How do I get my man to agree to more meatless meals?" The best way is to start with his favorite meals.

Brainstorm ways you can take the meat out and add something that can take its place. That way, you are delivering him the flavors he already likes and just making a few changes to make the meal without the standard ingredient.

**Ingredients**

For the Marinade

- ✓ 1/4 cup avocado oil
- ✓ 1/4 cup lime juice (juice from about 2 limes)
- ✓ 1 teaspoon dried oregano
- ✓ 1 teaspoon chili powder
- ✓ 1/2 teaspoon garlic powder
- ✓ 1/2 teaspoon sea salt
- ✓ 1/4 teaspoon pepper

For the Fajitas

- ✓ 5 portobello mushrooms
- ✓ 1 onion, sliced
- ✓ 1 green pepper, sliced
- ✓ 1 red pepper, sliced
- ✓ avocado oil
- ✓ salt and pepper
- ✓ 8 corn or whole grain tortillas, fajita sized

✓ Optional      Toppings/Additions: brown   rice,   shredded   cheese, guacamole,      sour      cream, tomatoes/salsa, etc.

## Instructions

1. Wash and dry your mushrooms. Gently de-stem them:  hold cap in one hand, and grab the stem with your dominate hand.  Gently twist the stem and pull away from the cap.
2. Slice the mushrooms and put in a large baking dish.
3. In a small bowl, mix together all of the ingredients for the marinade.  Pour the marinade over the sliced mushrooms. Use your hand to turn the mushrooms over so they are coated on all sides.

Cover with foil and let marinate for at least 30 minutes.

4. Heat the tortillas according to package directions and keep warm.

5. Preheat the oven to 400 degrees. Roast the mushrooms, covered for 15 minutes. Uncover and roast an additional 10 minutes.

6. While the mushrooms are roasting, heat some oil in a medium pan over medium heat. Add the onions and peppers and season with salt and pepper. Sauté until they are soft and starting to brown, about 10 minutes or so.

7. Serve the mushrooms and onion and pepper mixture on warm tortillas with the optional toppings you prefer. Enjoy!

notes

When I'm in a hurry, I've made these without the marinating time. They are still good, but I like the flavor better when they have time to marinate.

- Pantry Pumpkin Bisque

This Pantry Pumpkin Bisque is made with ingredients you probably have in your pantry! It's Paleo and Whole30 compliant, gluten-free, and easily adapted to be vegan.

With dinner options limited, I turned to my pantry. Thank goodness I keep it well-stocked. It doesn't matter what month it is when you're hungry, and besides, pumpkin always tastes good. Which would explain why I keep it stocked through the winter. If you don't keep it as a staple in your pantry, you should.

## Ingredients

- ✓ 1 onion, chopped
- ✓ 1 tablespoon coconut oil (you can substitute butter or olive oil if you prefer)
- ✓ 3-4 cups organic chicken stock
- ✓ 1 cup coconut milk
- ✓ 2 (15 ounce) cans pumpkin puree (not pumpkin pie mix)
- ✓ 1 1/2 teaspoons salt
- ✓ 2 teaspoons mild curry
- ✓ 1/2 teaspoon ground ginger
- ✓ 1/4 teaspoon ground cumin
- ✓ pinch (or more if you like things spicy) cayenne pepper {optional}
- ✓ pinch nutmeg

✓ generous amount of freshly ground black pepper

## Instructions

1. In a stock pot or dutch oven, heat the oil or butter over medium heat.
2. Add the onion and saute until soft and beginning to brown, about 5-6 minutes.
3. Add the chicken stock, coconut milk, pumpkin, and spices and bring to a simmer. Simmer for 5-10 minutes.
4. Transfer soup to a blender, in batches, and blend until smooth (you can also use an immersion blender if you have one). Return to pot and bring the temperature back up to hot.
5. Serve immediately.

Optional toppings: plain yogurt or parmesan cheese, pepitas

- Vegan Mexican Stuffed Peppers

These healthy Vegan Mexican Stuffed Peppers are bursting with bold flavor and are made in your slow cooker.

Total time: 3 hours 10 min

Serves: 4

**Ingredients**

- ✓ 2 cups cooked quinoa
- ✓ 2 1/2 cups salsa
- ✓ 1 cup corn kernels
- ✓ 1 (15 ounce) can black beans, drained and rinsed

- ✓ 2 teaspoons cumin
- ✓ 1 teaspoon ancho chili powder
- ✓ 1/2 teaspoon smoked paprika
- ✓ 1/2 teaspoon garlic salt
- ✓ 1/4 teaspoon salt
- ✓ 4 large bell peppers (any color), tops, seeds, and veins removed, and cut in half
- ✓ 1 very large or 2 smaller avocados
- ✓ juice from 1 lime
- ✓ 1/4 teaspoon salt
- ✓ 1/2 teaspoon hot sauce (optional)
- ✓ water
- ✓ 1/2 cup chopped cilantro
- ✓ lime wedges

## Instructions

1. In a large bowl, mix together the first 9 ingredients well.

2. Fill each pepper half with the quinoa mixture.
3. Place each pepper half in the slow cooker and cook on high for three hours.
4. While the peppers are cooking, prepare the avocado topping. Mash the avocado well in a bowl. Add the lime juice, hot sauce, and salt and whisk until very smooth. Add enough water to thin it to your preference (start with a teaspoon or so).
5. Serve the peppers with avocado sauce, chopped cilantro, and lime wedges.

- Roasted Vegetable Buddha Bowl

If you are looking for a warming, plant-powered bowl that tastes as good as it is nutritious, this is your recipe. A "Buddha Bowl" is basically a bowl of vegetables and such all mixed together, and it's pretty much my favorite way to eat vegetables.

Total time: 30 min

Serves: 2

**Ingredients**

- ✓ 1/2 pound brussels sprouts, rough end removed and cut into halves or fourths, depending on their size
- ✓ 4 rainbow carrots, sliced
- ✓ 1 small head broccoli, stems removed and florets cut into small pieces
- ✓ avocado oil (or oil of choice)
- ✓ salt and pepper
- ✓ 1 cup cooked brown rice
- ✓ FOR THE TAHINI LEMON SAUCE
- ✓ 1/4 cup tahini
- ✓ 1/4 cup water
- ✓ 5 tablespoons lemon juice
- ✓ 1 clove garlic, minced
- ✓ salt and pepper

## Instructions

1. Preheat the oven to 450 degrees.

2. Place your vegetables on a baking sheet and drizzle with oil. Sprinkle with salt and pepper and toss to coat.
3. Roast in the preheated oven until the vegetables are browned, about 20 minutes.
4. While the vegetables are roasting, make your sauce.
5. Place the tahini, water, lemon juice, and garlic in a blender and blend until smooth. Taste and add salt and pepper to taste.
6. When the vegetables are roasted, place the vegetables and rice in a bowl. Top with the dressing and toss to coat. Enjoy!

- Sweet Potato Noodles With 5-Minute Peanut Sauce

These sweet potato noodles make a fast, easy, and delicious dinner. The first time I saw sweet potato noodles, I was obsessed. I like zucchini noodles, but I like sweet potato noodles even more. How cool is it that you can make noodles with vegetables? Best food trend ever. Paired with a flavorful peanut sauce you can whip up in your blender, this meal is a winner.

Total time: 20 min

Serves: 4

## Ingredients

- ✓ 1/2 cup peanut butter
- ✓ 3/4 cup water
- ✓ 2 tablespoons tamari or soy sauce
- ✓ 1 teaspoon toasted sesame oil
  - o 1 1/2 inch thin slice fresh ginger, peeled and cut into small peices
- ✓ 2 large sweet potatoes, spiralized or cut into thin noodles
- ✓ 2 tablespoons extra virgin olive oil
- ✓ 1 small garlic clove, minced
- ✓ 1/4 cup peanuts, crushed
- ✓ 1/2 cup fresh cilantro, chopped

## Instructions

1. Put the first 5 ingredients (through ginger) in your blender and blend until smooth. Set aside.
2. In a large skillet, heat the olive oil over medium low heat. Add the garlic and sweet potato noodles. Using tongs, toss the noodles until they are covered in the oil. Cook just until all the noodles are hot, about 4-5 minutes.
3. Meanwhile, heat the sauce in a small saucepan over medium low heat until it is warm. (optional)
4. To serve, add 1/4 of the noodles to a plate, top with some of the sauce, and then top with some cilantro and the crushed peanuts. Enjoy!

- sweet potato black bean burger

These burgs are vegan and gluten-free (you'd need to get a gluten-free bun, of course) and 100% satisfying. All I think they need is a nice salad for a side dish and you've got yourself a meal. Add I hope you love them!

Total time: 20 min

Serves: 6

**Ingredients**

- ✓ 1 tablespoon ground flaxseed meal+3 tablespoons water (or 1 egg)
- ✓ 1 cup cooked mashed sweet potato (from 1 large or 2 smaller sweet potatoes)
- ✓ 1/2 cup cooked quinoa
- ✓ 1 (15 ounce) can black beans, drained and rinsed
- ✓ 1/4 cup loosely packed fresh chopped cilantro
- ✓ 1 teaspoon chili powder
- ✓ 1/2 teaspoon ground cumin
- ✓ 1/2 teaspoon oregano
- ✓ 1/8 teaspoon garlic salt
- ✓ 1/4 teaspoon salt
- ✓ 1 tablespoon lime juice
- ✓ oil (I like avocado oil for this)

## Instructions

1. Mix together your flaxseed meal and water and set it aside until it gels.
2. Place all ingredients in a bowl and mix well. Use a potato masher or the back of a large spoon to mash the beans, leaving a few in tact for texture.
3. In a large skillet, heat a thin layer of oil over medium high heat.
4. Form the sweet potato mixture into 6 patties.
5. When the skillet is hot enough to sizzle, add the patties, in batches if necessary. Cook on one side until a crispy exterior is formed, about 5-7 minutes.
6. Carefully flip each patty and cook an additional 5 minutes on the second side.

7. Serve with your favorite toppings like guacamole. Enjoy!

- grilled vegetables with pasta

It's so easy to transform fresh vegetables into a filling and delicious vegetarian meal. I use whole wheat pasta as much as I can get away with it, but use whatever your family prefers. This vegetarian dinner comes together in a snap.

Total time: 40 min

Serves: 6

**Ingredients**

- ✓ 1 bunch of asparagus, tough ends removed and cut into 2-inch pieces
- ✓ 2 large zucchinis, cut in half length wise and then sliced
- ✓ 1 bell pepper, seeds removed and then cut into 2-inch pieces
- ✓ 1/4 of a large onion, diced
- ✓ 1/4 cup avocado oil (or oil of choice, preferably a high-heat oil)
- ✓ 1 teaspoon dried thyme
- ✓ 1/2 teaspoon coarse sea salt
- ✓ 1/4 teaspoon freshly ground black pepper
- ✓ 12 ounces whole wheat spaghetti
- ✓ 1/4 cup grated parmesan cheese
- ✓ 2 tablespoons butter
- ✓ 2 tablespoons extra-virgin olive oil
- ✓ 8-9 fresh basil leaves, cut into thin strips

## Instructions

1. Preheat your grill to medium heat, about 400-425 degrees.
2. Put all of your cut vegetables into a large bowl and add the avocado oil, thyme, salt and pepper. Toss to evenly coat with the oil and seasonings. Transfer the vegetables to a grill pan. Put the pan directly on the grill grates and close the grill.
3. Cook until the vegetables are tender and charred, about 20-30 minutes. Toss the vegetables 2-3 times during the grilling time to ensure they grill evenly.
4. Meanwhile, put your spaghetti in a large pot and fill with water. Add 1 tablespoon salt to the water.

Bring to a boil and cook according to package directions. Before you drain the spaghetti, reserve 1 cup of the cooking water (you won't need quite that much, but it's better to have too much than not enough). Drain the pasta and do not rinse.

5. Put the pasta back into the pot and add the olive oil, butter, and a few tablespoons of the pasta water. Stir until the butter is melted.

6. Add the cooked vegetables to the pot and toss them around so they are evenly incorporated into the pasta (sometimes I use tongs to do this).

7. Add the parmesan cheese and a few more tablespoons of the cooking water. Add more water if

the pasta seems too dry; I usually add about 1/2 cup total. Top with the fresh basil and serve immediately.

8. Enjoy!

- Coconut curry chickpea lentil soup

Marriage is all about compromise. I'm sure you've heard that phrase about a million times, especially if you are married. As cliche as it may be, it's true. You have to be able to bend and stretch; being rigid doesn't get you very far.

So let's talk about compromising at dinner time. This has been a big adjustment for me in marriage. Before you're married, you get to eat whatever you want for dinner–you follow your cravings and desires. Once you're married (and have kids, but that's a whole different post...) you have to consider someone else's stomach and taste buds when you're deciding what to have for dinner. Easy if your food likes and dislikes line up. Not so easy if they don't.

This soup is hearty and comforting, yet low calorie. Each serving has just 228 calories and boasts 12 grams of protein! It's a healthy, easy recipe that is full of flavor. You can't go wrong with that combo!

Total time: 4 hours

Serves: 7

**Ingredients**

- ✓ 2 (15 ounce) cans chickpeas (garbanzo beans), drained and rinsed
- ✓ 1 cup dry lentils, picked over and rinsed
- ✓ 1 large sweet potato, cut into small cubes
- ✓ 1 (15 ounce) can lite coconut milk
- ✓ 2 tablespoons curry powder (I used mild curry)
- ✓ 1 teaspoon ground turmeric
- ✓ 1 teaspoon ground ginger
- ✓ 1/2 teaspoon salt
- ✓ 1/4 teaspoon pepper
- ✓ 6 cups vegetable broth

## Instructions

1. Put all ingredients in the slow cooker and mix well. Cook on high heat for 4 hours. (I have not

tried it, but cooking it on low heat for 8 hours would most likely work also.) Taste and add more salt and pepper if you prefer. Enjoy!

- Sweet potato and black bean chili

I'm in love with this sweet potato and black bean chili because of its bold flavor, but I can't ignore that it's also a super easy recipe. The hardest thing you have to do is chop an onion and some sweet potatoes. You can handle that, right? I think you're going to love this chili, so I hope you give it a try!

Total time: 44 min

Serves: 6

**Ingredients**

- ✓ 1 tablespoon extra virgin olive oil
- ✓ 1 onion, diced
- ✓ 3 cloves garlic, minced
- ✓ 2 medium-large sweet potatoes, peeled and cubed
- ✓ 1 1/2 tablespoons ancho chili powder
- ✓ 2 teaspoons ground cumin powder
- ✓ 1 teaspoon salt
- ✓ 1/4 teaspoon pepper
- ✓ 1/4 teaspoon smoked paprika
- ✓ 1/4 teaspoon ground cinnamon
- ✓ 1 (15 ounce) can diced fire-roasted tomatoes

- ✓ 3-4 cups chicken or vegetable stock
- ✓ 2 tablespoons tomato paste
- ✓ 2 (15 ounce) cans black beans, drained and rinsed
- ✓ Optional
- ✓ fresh cilantro
- ✓ lime wedges

## Instructions

2. Heat the olive oil over medium heat.
3. Add the onion and cook until softened and lightly browned, about 5-7 minutes.
4. Add the garlic and cook one more minutes.
5. Next, add the sweet potato, chili powder, cumin, salt, pepper, smoked paprika, and cinnamon.

Stir until the sweet potatoes are coated with the spices.

6. Next, add the diced fire-roasted tomatoes, 3 cups of the stock, and the tomato paste. Bring it to a boil, and then reduce the heat and allow the mixture to simmer until the potatoes are soft, about 30 minutes.

7. Stir in the black beans and cook until they are warmed, a few minutes more.

8. If the chili is too thick for your preference, add another cup of stock.

9. Serve with fresh cilantro and lime wedges. <——Although optional, I highly recommend using the cilantro and lime! The cilantro and

lime juice compliments and balances the flavors nicely. Enjoy!

- Beet burgers

These beet burgers are hearty, filling, and have great texture. They aren't mushy at all, like so many veggie/bean burgers can be. They are slightly delicate, but hold together well once cooked.

If you try these I hope you love them as much as I do!

Total time: 30 min

Serves: 8

## Ingredients

- ✓ 1-2 tablespoons olive oil or coconut oil
- ✓ 1 medium yellow onion, diced
- ✓ 3 garlic cloves, minced
- ✓ 3 medium beets, peeled and then grated or shredded
- ✓ 1/2 cup rolled oats or walnuts
- ✓ 1/2 cup prunes
- ✓ 2 eggs
- ✓ 1 (15 ounce) can black beans, drained and rinsed
- ✓ 2 cups cooked brown rice
- ✓ 2 teaspoons coriander
- ✓ 1 teaspoon thyme
- ✓ 1 teaspoon salt
- ✓ 1/4 teaspoon cinnamon
- ✓ 1/8 teaspoon black pepper
- ✓ 1 tablespoon miso (optional)

✓ oil for frying (optional)

**Instructions**

1. In a large skillet, heat the oil and then add the diced onion and cook until soft, about 5 minutes. Add the garlic and cook another minute. Turn off the heat and set aside.

2. {Meanwhile, grate or shred your beets. I use my food processor shredding attachment and love how easy it is!} In your food processor, pulse the prunes and oats or walnuts until they are well combined, but not so much they are turning into a paste. Add the eggs and process until they are just combined. {Alternatively, you can crush/chop the walnuts and

chop the prunes and then mix in the egg. I just really like the convenience of the food processor.} Set aside.

3. In a large bowl, mash your beans until they are mostly mashed, but a few beans are still in tact. Add the beats, prune/walnut/egg mixture, onion and garlic mixture, brown rice, coriander, thyme, salt, cinnamon, pepper, and miso. Mix very well until everything is well combined.

4. Form your mixture into 8 patties. Thinner patties cook better, so flatten them with your hands. Now you have 2 options for cooking.

5. Frying option: Heat some oil in a large skillet and cook the patties

for 4-6 minutes per side. Be careful when flipping.

6. Baking option: Bake the patties in a 375 degree oven for 30-40 minutes, carefully flipping once half way through the cooking time.

## Notes

*If the burgers fall apart a little when you flip them, just form them back together carefully with your hands or the spatula. They will hold together better when they are fully cooked.

- Zucchini Noodles With Chunky Tomato Sauce And Bean Balls

Zucchini noodles, paired with a chunky tomato sauce and bean balls makes for a light, healthy summer-time meal that is vegan and gluten-free. Zucchini noodles (zoodles) are easy to make with an inexpensive julienne slicer.

Total time: 40 min

Serves: 6

**Ingredients**

✓ 12 small or 6 large zucchinis

- ✓ For the tomato sauce
- ✓ 1 tablespoon organic refined coconut oil, or oil of choice
- ✓ 1 large onion, chopped
- ✓ 6 cloves garlic, minced
- ✓ 2 portobello mushroom caps, chopped
- ✓ 1 (28 ounce) can diced tomatoes
- ✓ 1 (15 1/2 ounce) can tomato sauce
- ✓ 1/2 teaspoon salt
- ✓ 1/4 teaspoon freshly ground black pepper
- ✓ 1 tablespoon dried oregano
- ✓ 1 teaspoon marjoram
- ✓ 1 cup fresh basil, chopped
- ✓ For the bean balls
- ✓ 2 (15 ounce) cans black beans, drained and rinsed
- ✓ 2/3 cup rolled oats
- ✓ 4 tablespoons tomato paste

- ✓ 2 tablespoons nutritional yeast (parmesan cheese may be substituted)
- ✓ 3 tablespoons Italian seasoning blend
- ✓ 1/4 teaspoon salt

## Instructions

1. Preheat the oven to 350 degrees.
2. Make zucchini noodles by using a julienne slicer (or a spiralizer if you prefer). Set aside in a large bowl.
3. To make your sauce, start by heating the oil in a large stock pot or Dutch oven.
4. Cook the onion and garlic until soft, about 5 minutes.
5. Add the chopped mushroom and allow to cook another 10 minutes.

6. Stir in the tomatoes, tomato sauce, oregano, marjoram, salt, and pepper. Allow to simmer for 15 minutes. Stir in the fresh basil.

7. While your mushrooms are cooking during the sauce-making, start making your bean balls. Put your beans into a large bowl and mash (I use a potato masher for this). It's okay to have a few beans in tact.

8. Add the rest of the ingredients and stir well. Use your hand to knead the mixture together, making sure the ingredients are well incorporated.

9. Roll the bean mixture into 1 1/2 inch balls and place them on a baking sheet that is either lightly coated with oil or lined with

parchment paper. You will get about 28-30 balls.

10.     Bake in the preheated oven for 16-18 minutes, turning once halfway through the cooking time.

11.     To serve, place a serving of zucchini noodles on a plate, top with 4-6 meatballs, and finally cover it all with the tomato sauce. If you aren't vegan and can enjoy dairy, feel free to top it with some freshly grated parmesan cheese. Enjoy!

- One Pot Coconut Curry Lentil Bowl With Chickpeas And Kale

This Coconut Curry Lentil Bowl is a one-pot dinner that comes together in about 30 minutes. This vegan, gluten-free meal is full of flavor and is immensely satisfying. It pairs perfectly with warm naan bread.

Total time: 30 min

Serves: 4

**Ingredients**

✓ 3/4 cup red lentils

- ✓ 1 (15 1/2) ounce can diced tomatoes with garlic and onion with juices (I blended mine a little to avoid big tomato chunks that my family dislikes, but that is optional)
- ✓ 1 (15 1/2) can lite coconut milk
- ✓ 1 cup water or vegetable broth
- ✓ 1 heaping tablespoon curry powder
- ✓ ~1 1/2 inch piece of fresh ginger, minced
- ✓ 1 teaspoon turmeric
- ✓ 1 teaspoon salt
- ✓ 1 (15 1/2 oz.) can chickpeas, drained and rinsed
- ✓ 4 cups roughly chopped, deveined kale
- ✓ 1 tablespoon lime juice

✓ 1/3 cup roughly chopped fresh cilantro

## Instructions

1. In a Dutch oven or large high-sided skillet, combine the red lentils, tomatoes with their juices, coconut milk, water or broth, curry powder, ginger, turmeric, and salt.
2. Bring the mixture to a boil, then reduce the heat, cover, and simmer for about 18 minutes.
3. Stir in the chickpeas and kale and allow to cook another 3-5 minutes, until the kale is wilted and bright green.
4. Stir in the lime and cilantro and serve. Enjoy!

- quinoa patties with black beans and corn

These Quinoa Patties with Black Beans and Corn are the BEST vegan patties ever. They hold together well and are full of flavor. Quinoa+Black Beans=tons of protein. Easy, clean-eating recipe.

Total time: 30 min

Serves: 8

**Ingredients**

- ✓ 1 cup quinoa, rinsed and drained/dried well
- ✓ 2 cups water
- ✓ 8-10 basil leaves, chopped
- ✓ 1 1/2 cup cooked black beans (or 1-15 ounce can, drained and rinsed)
- ✓ 1 cup frozen corn kernels, thawed
- ✓ 1 teaspoon kosher salt
- ✓ freshly ground black pepper
- ✓ 1 tablespoon fresh lime juice
- ✓ 1/8 teaspoon garlic powder
- ✓ 1/2 cup cornmeal
- ✓ grapeseed oil, for frying (or oil of choice)
- ✓ avocado slices (optional)
- ✓ lime wedges (optional)

## Instructions

1. Put the quinoa and water in a pot and bring to a boil. Reduce the heat and cover. Cook until the water is absorbed, about 15 minutes. Remove from heat and allow the quinoa to cool slightly.
2. To the cooled quinoa, add the basil leaves, black beans, corn, salt, a few turns of freshly ground black pepper, lime juice, and garlic powder. Mix well. Then, with a potato masher, mash the mixture together. Slowly add the cornmeal until you have a stiff mixture.
3. Cover a large skillet pan with a thin layer of oil and heat the oil over medium high heat. Form the mixture into 2″ balls (smaller for

nuggets). Flatten the balls and fry in the oil 3-4 minutes per side.

4. Serve with avocado slices and lime wedges, if desired. Enjoy!

## PLANT BASED SMOOTHIES

Smoothies are awesome. They're quick. They're easy. They're whole-body nourishing. And they're so modifiable! You can make them more desserty, or more proteiny. With greens, without greens. Banana, no banana. Dairy, no dairy. I have organzed 5 of our favorite recipes and organized them so that the simpler recipes are at the top for those who are newer to a plant-based diet.

- Creamy Chocolate Breakfast Shake

A creamy vegan chocolate shake with tons of fruit, protein, and rich chocolate flavor. Makes the perfect late-night dessert.

Total time: 10 min

Serves: 2

**Ingredients**

- ✓ 2 frozen ripe bananas (chopped prior to freezing)
- ✓ 1/3 cup frozen strawberries (or blueberries)
- ✓ 2-3 heaping Tbsp cocoa powder

- ✓ 2 Tbsp salted almond butter*
- ✓ 1 Tbsp flaxseed meal (optional)
- ✓ 1.5-2 cups unsweetened vanilla almond milk (sub soy or coconut)
- ✓ 1 dash stevia or agave nectar (depending on sweetness of bananas)
- ✓ 1/3 cup ice
- ✓ 1 big handful big handful of spinach

## Instructions

1. Place all ingredients in a blender and blend until smooth.
2. If you prefer a more chocolatey shake, add more cocoa powder. If you prefer it sweeter, add more stevia or agave. If you prefer it thinner, add less ice OR more almond milk.

- Hide Your Kale Smoothie

A nutrient-packed berry smoothie that's sweet and creamy and hides the taste and texture of kale! The perfect healthy breakfast, post-workout meal, or afternoon snack.

Total time: 5 min

Serves: 2

**Ingredients**

- ✓ 1 medium ripe banana (previously peeled, sliced and frozen // 1 banana yields ~3/4 cup)

- ✓ 1/2 cup frozen mixed berries (or sub blueberries)
- ✓ 1 heaping Tbsp hulled hemp seeds (organic if possible)
- ✓ 2 cups frozen or fresh kale (any kind)
- ✓ 2/3 cup 100% pomegranate juice
- ✓ 3/4-1 1/2 cups filtered water

## Instructions

1. Add all ingredients to a blender and blend until smooth, adding more water as needed. Taste and adjust flavors as needed. Add more banana or some agave for added sweetness.
2. Serve immediately – enough for 2.

## Notes

*Pomegranate juice really makes this recipe and seems to hide the kale best. I've tried it with orange and cherry and they didn't do the job quite as well! Use substitute as you see fit.

*Adding a bit of almond milk ups the creaminess.

*1 Tbsp of almond butter would add even more staying power.

*Nutrition information is a rough estimate.

- Hidden Greens Chocolate Protein Shake

This smoothie calls for 2 tablespoons of hemp hearts which provide a huge nutritional boost to this smoothie, including more than 6 grams of complete protein, as well as omega-3 fatty acids, magnesium, and more. Hemp hearts, kale, and dates require a strong blender to blend them smooth (a Vitamix blends them into a super creamy shake). If your blender can't blend the hemp hearts, kale, or dates smooth, I recommend swapping out the hemp for a serving of your favourite protein powder and swapping the dates for pure maple syrup (otherwise, you'll just have a grainy end result). You can also swap the kale for baby spinach as it blends easier.

Total time: 5 min

Serves: 3

## Ingredients

- ✓ 1 1/2 cups unsweetened almond milk
- ✓ 1 cup frozen organic kale
- ✓ 2 to 3 pitted large Medjool dates, to taste*
- ✓ 2 tablespoons hulled hemp seed
- ✓ 2 tablespoons unsweetened cocoa powder
- ✓ 1 large frozen banana

✓ Dash of cinnamon
✓ 1 tablespoon avocado (for thickening)
✓ Ice, if desired

## Instruction

1. Add all ingredients into a high-speed blender and blend until smooth. Adjust sweetness to taste, if desired.

## Tips:

\* If your dates are dry or stiff, I recommend soaking the pitted dates in boiled water for a half hour and then draining well before use.

- Blueberry Maple Protein Shake

This simple recipe requires less than 10 and comes together in about 5 minutes. It's the perfect portable breakfast that provides a full serving of fruit and plenty of protein.

Total time: 5 min

Serves: 1

## Ingredients

2. 1/2 cup cottage cheese or low-fat yogurt (I use a mix of the two)*
3. 3 Tbsp vanilla protein powder

4. 1/2 cup frozen blueberries

5. 1/4 - 1/2 tsp maple extract

6. 1/4 tsp vanilla extract

7. 2 tsp flaxseed meal

8. Sweetener of choice (to taste)

9. 10-15 ice cubes

10.   1/4 cup water

11.   Instructions

12.   Place all of your ingredients in a blender and mix until well combined. If it appears too runny, add more ice. If it's too thick, add more water. Add more sweetener or extract at the end if the flavor isn't strong enough for your taste.

## Notes

*Use a non-dairy yogurt or milk for the base and a non-dairy protein powder to easily make this recipe vegan-friendly.

*I add a handful of raw spinach to mine for extra veggies without any change in flavor.

- Chocolate Strawberry Almond Protein Smoothie

This chocolate strawberry almond protein smoothie looks like a typical green smoothie, but it's not. Not only does it have strawberries, but also almonds and superfoods. And, it's vegan, gluten-free, dairy-free, soy-free, and has no refined sugars.

Total time: 5 min

Serves: 1-2

**Ingredients**

- ✓ 1 1/2 cup homemade almond milk
- ✓ 1 cup organic strawberries
- ✓ 1 scoop chocolate protein powder
- ✓ 1/4 cup organic raw almonds
- ✓ 1 tablespoon organic coconut oil
- ✓ 1 tablespoon organic maca powder
- ✓ 1 tablespoon organic hemp seeds

## For Garnish:

- ✓ organic hemp seeds
- ✓ organic cacao nibs

## Instructions

1. Put all ingredients into a blender and blend until well combined.
2. Optional: garnish with organic hemp seeds or organic cacao nibs.
3. Enjoy!

## Notes

Tip #1: I like to make my own homemade almond milk with my Vitamix to avoid the additives and processed boxed milk, but you can substitute it your favorite non-dairy (or dairy for non-vegan) milk. I buy my raw, organic, unpasteurized, sproutable almonds in bulk from here.

Tip #2: The organic hemp seeds and organic cacao nibs for garnish are optional and added for extra nutrition. Tip #3: You can use fresh or frozen strawberries...I like to use frozen so I don't have to add ice cubes.

# CONCLUSION

As far as how strict your plant-based diet should be, it's really a matter of which of the philosophies you follow and how hard-core you are about personal food philosophy.

Is total veganism the only true plant-based diet? Are vegetarians who eat a little fish and perhaps the occasional red meat dish (gasp) going to vegetarian hell?

It's a personal choice, but here's my take - you won't find many diets out there that don't admit grubbing down on more of those good ole' fresh fruits and veggies and cutting back on the red meat while lowering your calories won't do wonders for your health, your looks, and your waistline.

Be aware of these benefits and take them very seriously.

But before you get too drastic with your new diet plan, acknowledge that a successful diet is a balance between personal priorities, quality of life, and health. And it's completely possible to take up a predominantly plant-based diet without signing over your soul to the veggie garden and completely outlawing cheeseburgers for the rest of your life.

A good diet is maintained through basic guidelines, and an occasional cheat from time to time (once you've got it under control) doesn't make you a bad person or mean you're a traitor of some vague, esoteric clan. After you've established solid eating habits, cheating can even be a good thing sometimes.

Sure, there's a lot of research out there raising some very interesting questions about meat and the potential damage it can do to our bodies (especially in high quantities), but more research is still needed before any absolutes are determined. Meanwhile, just use some common sense.

Michael Pollan probably puts it best in his book, "In Defense of Food," when he sums up his own rules for plant-eating as such: "Eat food. Not too much. Mostly plants."

It doesn't' get any simpler than that, and any person out there looking to reap the health and weight loss benefits of a sensible plant-based diet without putting themselves through raw broccoli boot camp would do well to follow his simple philosophy.

Arming yourself with knowledge, based on fact, about nutrition, dieting and exercise is vital if you are serious about losing weight, keeping it off and living a healthier lifestyle.

39009977R00135

Made in the USA
Middletown, DE
13 March 2019